THE MACHIAVELLIAN ENTERPRISE

Leo Paul S. de Alvarez

THE
MACHIAVELLIAN
ENTERPRISE

A Commentary on *The Prince*

NORTHERN ILLINOIS

UNIVERSITY

PRESS

DEKALB 1999

JC
143
.M3946
D37
1999

© 1999 by Northern Illinois University Press

Published by the Northern Illinois

University Press, DeKalb, Illinois 60115

Manufactured in the United States

using acid-free paper

Design by Julia Fauci

Library of Congress

Cataloging-in-Publication Data

De Alvarez, Leo Paul S.

The Machiavellian enterprise /

Leo Paul S. de Alvarez.

p.   cm.

Includes bibliographical references.

ISBN 0-87580-247-8 (alk. paper)

1. Machiavelli, Niccolò, 1469–1527.

Principe. I. Title.

JC143.M3946D37   1999

320.1—dc21   98-54214

CIP

CONTENTS

Preface vii

Acknowledgments xi

The Epistle Dedicatory 3

PART ONE: OF PRINCIPATES

I.	How Many Kinds of Principates There Are and by What Modes They Are Acquired 9
II.	Of Hereditary Principates 12
III.	Of Mixed Principates 13
IV.	Why the Kingdom of Darius Which Alexander Had Seized Did Not Rebel against His Successors after the Death of Alexander 19
V.	In What Mode Cities or Principates Must Be Administered Which before They Were Seized Used to Live by Their Own Laws 22
VI.	Of New Principates Which by One's Arms and Virtue Are Acquired 25
VII.	Of New Principates Which by the Arms of Others and Fortune Are Acquired 32
VIII.	Of Those Who through Wickednesses Attain to the Principate 36
IX.	Of the Civil Principate 42
X.	In What Mode the Strengths of All Principates Ought to Be Weighed 46
XI.	Of Ecclesiastical Principates 48

PART TWO: OF ARMS

XII.	How Many Kinds of Militia There Are and about Mercenary Soldiers 55
XIII.	Of Soldiers: Auxiliaries, Mixed and One's Own 60
XIV.	What a Prince Should Do about the Militia 64

PART THREE: OF THE QUALITIES OF THE PRINCE

XV.   Of Those Things for Which Men, and Especially Princes,
       Are Praised or Blamed   75

XVI.   Of Liberality and Parsimony   79

XVII. Of Cruelty and Pity: And If It Is Better to Be Loved Than Feared,
       or the Contrary   82

XVIII. In What Mode Princes Ought to Keep Faith   85

XIX.   Of Avoiding Contempt and Hatred   90

PART FOUR: OF THE PRUDENCE OF THE PRINCE

XX.   If Fortresses and Many Other Things Which Everyday
       Are Employed by Princes Are Useful or Useless   103

XXI.   What a Prince Should Do That He May Be Esteemed   109

XXII. Of Those Whom Princes Have as Secretaries   113

XXIII. In What Mode Flatterers Are to Be Avoided   115

XXIV. Why the Princes of Italy Have Lost Their Kingdom   117

XXV.   How Much Fortune Is Able to Do in Human Things and in
       What Mode One May Oppose Her   125

XXVI. Exhortation to Lay Hold of Italy and Vindicate Her Liberty
       from the Barbarians   131

       CONCLUSION: On the Order of the Argument in *The Prince*   137

       Index   141

PREFACE

The following commentary is based on the promise by Machiavelli that *The Prince* enables one to understand all that he has come to know. In his *Discourses on the First Ten Books of Titus Livy,* Machiavelli declares that he has expressed in it all that he has learned through practice and reading. The *Discourses,* as one would expect, is then more comprehensive than *The Prince.* He does not express all that he knows in *The Prince;* it will, however, shorten the time needed for our examination of, and reflection on, his thought.

It has long been said that *The Prince* does not develop an argument but rather presents an episodic set of reflections. In working out the meaning of each chapter, however, I believe that a very carefully crafted argument emerges, one seen most clearly in the relationship of one chapter to another. No commentaries have sought simply to see what the work itself presents, to follow the argument chapter by chapter, without attempting to bring in arguments and themes from external texts. Thus I wish to give a reading of the text itself—to see what results from reading without preconceptions, as if one had accidentally come across the work and had no notion of the author, his reputation, or any opinions about him.

The method I have followed necessarily means that in the earlier chapters questions are raised and that only in subsequent chapters are we given clues to the answers. Puzzling references and allusions are later clarified, and the significance of earlier topics becomes evident only toward the end of the book. I attempt, in short, to present a first reading of *The Prince.*

Machiavelli's first chapter lists thirteen kinds of principates:

1. ALL THE STATES AND DOMINIONS
    a. Republics
    b. Principates
        (1). Hereditary principates (chapter II)
        (2). New principates
            (a). Wholly new principates (chapter VI)
            (b). Mixed principates (chapter III)

2. ACQUIRED DOMINIONS (character of)
    a. Acquired principates (chapter IV)
    b. Acquired republics (chapter V)

3. ACQUIRED DOMINIONS (manner of acquisition)
    a. By the arms of others; that is, fortune (chapter VII)
    b. By one's own arms; that is, virtue (chapter VI)

One notices that when a state is acquired it becomes a dominion, which is to say, it becomes subject to the mastery of a lord.[1]

Machiavelli does not, however, weave his argument exactly in this order. The actual order of his discussion is:

1. PRINCIPATES
    a. Hereditary principates (chapter II)
    b. Mixed principates (chapter III)
        (1). Prince and slaves (chapter IV)
        (2). Prince and barons (chapter IV)
        (3). Free dominions (cities) (chapter V)
    c. Wholly new principates
        (1). Founded by one's own arms and virtue (chapter VI)
        (2). Founded by the arms of others and fortune (chapter VII)
        (3). Founded by criminal means (chapter VIII)
        (4). Founded by lawful means (chapter IX)
    d. How to judge the strength of principates (chapter X)
    e. Ecclesiastical principates (chapter XI)

Machiavelli is far more radical, simple, and even shocking in the distinctions he first makes than he later actually proves to be. He first makes a sharp distinction between principates and republics, but then he adds a new category of a prince and his barons. Initially he does not allude to the difference between criminal and lawful means of acquiring principates, but then he unexpectedly brings it up in chapters VIII and IX. He makes no mention of the possibility of spiritual power but rather speaks generally of that which has imperium or power over men. Then he explicitly brings up in chapter XI the possibility of a spiritual or invisible power. A greater variety of regimes is presented than is first indicated.

The actual order of discussion still includes thirteen topics. Chapter XV marks the beginning of a new discussion, which concludes in chapter XIX. Machiavelli does not say in chapter XX, as he does in chapters XII and XV, that he is beginning another discussion, but it is evident that he is now concerned with a different matter: how a prince may with prudence maintain himself. He begins this discussion by listing precepts as to what princes are to do and make.[2] He ends this discussion in chapter XXV. The work therefore seems to be divided into four main parts, of which chapter I prepares the reader only for the first:

Part 1: Of Principates

Part 2: Of Arms

Part 3: Of the Qualities of the Prince

Part 4: Of the Prudence of the Prince

The Epistle Dedicatory and chapter XXVI frame the body of the text within the theme of the Medici and the possible liberation of Italy. What Machiavelli promises is a discussion of the kinds or natures of principates and how they may be founded and preserved. He promises, in other words, a theoretical discussion of regimes. Although his upsetting of his own order may warn us to be wary of Machiavellian promises, does he not fulfill his promise, but in an unexpected way? Throughout *The Prince* unexpected digressions appear that are crucial to the understanding of the argument. If Machiavelli disorders his own plan, perhaps it is because he wishes to indicate that the apparent order does not reflect the authentic argument of the book. The reader is therefore forced to discover Machiavelli's true intent.

NOTES

1. *Dominion* is used again in chapters II.8–9 and XXIV.14 of *The Prince*. References to passages in *The Prince* will be to chapters and pages of my translation of Niccolò Machiavelli, *The Prince* (Prospect Heights, Ill.: Waveland Press, 1989).

2. Sydney Anglo has called the section comprising chapters XX–XXIV a collection of "mere rag-bags of largely unrelated precepts" (*Machiavelli: A Dissection* [New York: Harcourt, Brace and World, 1969], 73).

ACKNOWLEDGMENTS

This book emerged out of the questions that left me puzzled in D. Malcolm Brown's political theory class at the University of California, Santa Barbara. I was fortunate that, soon after, Willmoore Kendall, at Stanford University, introduced me to Leo Strauss's *Thoughts on Machiavelli,* which gave me for the first time a guide for beginning the study of Machiavelli.

I have profited greatly from seminars that George Anastaplo gave at the University of Dallas, and I am especially indebted to him for the discussion of chapter XV. I obviously have also learned much from Harvey C. Mansfield, who was, as usual, very helpful especially in rethinking and revising parts of my translation of *The Prince.* I am grateful to Ms. Vicki Murray, of the University of Dallas, who proofread and corrected the first drafts of this commentary. I wish also to thank the Earhart Foundation of Ann Arbor, Michigan, for providing a summer grant to work upon this commentary. I am also very grateful to Larry Arnhart, of Northern Illinois University, for pushing me to publication.

My wife, Helen, has shared to a considerable degree in this work, as with the translation. Every aspect was discussed with her, from questions of grammar and style to the difficulties of interpreting certain passages.

Finally, I wish to thank the students of my classes, on whom these ideas were first tested, and whose questions and comments sharpened my study and understanding of *The Prince.*

THE MACHIAVELLIAN ENTERPRISE

THE EPISTLE DEDICATORY

Machiavelli begins with what is usual (the first word of the treatise is *Sogliono* [They usually]), although he then indicates that he cannot do the usual. He implies that his gifts or talents, as well as his fortune, are extremely limited and may prevent him from doing the usual. The appearance of conventionality, however, marks the entire work. The dedication appears to be the conventional address of a courtier to his prince, and it follows the form of the traditional book on the governance of a prince. Machiavelli seems to be following the long tradition of scholars who submit a "mirror of a prince" to a new prince. The Latin titles add to this effect: the title of the book is conventional, but the body of the text is in the vulgar tongue, which is most unconventional or novel. He begins with the usual but immediately departs from it.

We begin, then, with what is usually done by those who desire to acquire. In this case, they desire the favor of a prince, and to acquire it they bring what they themselves hold dear or what they see delights him the most. They assume that what they hold dear will be similarly regarded by the prince. Is there not, thus, an equality between the petitioners and the prince? Now the prince's favor is a grace or gift, not necessarily something the petitioners deserve; that is, it may not be justice that they desire.

What delights the prince the most, it would seem, are things that enhance his magnificence, that display his power and sumptuousness. In the second paragraph, Machiavelli speaks of the "pompous and magnificent words" usually employed by writers—presumably the writers of books for the government of princes. Such books are full of "artifice and extrinsic ornaments," whereas he wishes his book to be honored for its intrinsic qualities. Machiavelli uses a form of the word *ornament* three times in one sentence, twice as a verb and once as a noun: *ornata, ornamento, ornare*. We note that he again speaks of the "they" who "usually" do these things. What Machiavelli regards with contempt is that which is usually expected and therefore given.

Ornaments are tokens of a self-sufficient plenitude. Magnificence is the virtue of rightly spending great sums on the beautiful. The magnificent—Lorenzo is distinguished by that epithet—display their freedom from necessity by their love of the beautiful. In contrast, Machiavelli's gift is the best of his "equipment"; it is thus something useful.[1]

Not only does Machiavelli attack magnificence as a dubious virtue, he also declares, in the next sentence, that he, Machiavelli, knows something the prince does not. Machiavelli knows the high places; the prince, the low. The prince, therefore, does not know well the nature of princes; which is to say, he does not know himself. What the prince does not know, then, is how to rule, for not to know how princes act is not to know how to rule.

The unusual deed that Machiavelli performs is to offer to princes that which they need. He suggests thereby that magnificence, the title and the virtue alike, is a sham. A magnificent man pretends not to be in need; his concern is with the beautiful and not with the needful or the useful. Machiavelli seems to think that all men, high or low, are in need; man's true condition is one of desiring and therefore of needing. Machiavelli, here at the beginning, seems to indicate that human beings are equal in one respect, perhaps the decisive one: they are all desiring and therefore in need.

Machiavelli promises that his gift will "enable you"—he appears to be referring to Lorenzo—"in a very short time to understand all that I, in so many years and in so many of my hardships and dangers have come to know and understand." What Lorenzo, however, will find in the book is not so much knowledge as the testimony of Machiavelli's desire to serve him. (The word used is *servitù*, and it is subsequently always used in the text to indicate a state of slavery or servitude.) What Lorenzo will see in the book dedicated to him is that Machiavelli will be a loyal minister who will never think about himself but only of the greatness of the prince. Lorenzo is not said to be capable of grasping the useful teaching of the work. Instead, his outstanding quality is his fortune. Machiavelli is silent about Lorenzo's virtues throughout both the Epistle and the work as a whole. The duke is promised greatness by his fortune and other qualities; Machiavelli, in contrast, suffers under a great and continuous malignity of fortune. Fortune has favored the Medici; it has taken a great and continuous malignity of fortune to bring Machiavelli low. One notices a little later that a natural prince can lose his state as the consequence of an "extraordinary and excessive force." In contrast, the exemplar of a usurper, or "unnatural" prince, Cesare Borgia, is afflicted by an "extraordinary and extreme malignity of fortune." Does the continuousness of the malignity of fortune indicate that Machiavelli faces the most difficult circumstances of all? Moreover, what kind of a prince is he? Is the principal difference between Lorenzo and Machiavelli the difference in fortune?

The question must be raised because a reversal occurs in the second sentence of the Epistle Dedicatory. We see Machiavelli as one of the many who seek the favor of the prince, for he is, as they are, a man who desires to acquire. He is desirous, he says, of offering himself in servitude to "that"—the understood reference is "that Magnificence of Yours." Then the reversal occurs. In the first part of the sentence many are described as approaching one, the prince; but then the prince suddenly becomes the many princes who are now approached by one, Machiavelli, who brings his useful gift. Is not Machiavelli now the one who knows how to rule? Can only those who are on high understand the low and only those who are low understand those on high? If so, no one could understand himself, neither those who rule nor those who are ruled. Knowledge of the whole is thus not possible. Machiavelli, however, seems to imply that he has knowledge of the whole. He does not say that he knows only of the actions of great men; he says instead that there is nothing he holds more dear or with more esteem than that knowledge. Does he also know the people?

Is there not more than a hint of a revolutionary teaching in the Epistle Dedicatory? For if Lorenzo is not the true addressee of the book, then one must wonder who can be given "the faculty of being able to understand" all that Machiavelli has learned. Are these to replace the Lorenzos or those who are favored by fortune? Would not this signify that knowledge is to become the new basis for rule? Would not that be Machiavelli's triumph over fortune?

The dedication of *The Prince* to Lorenzo de' Medici presents Machiavelli in the conventional and therefore acceptable guise of a humble courtier. The guise of the loyal, supplicant courtier is disarming. Such a man is to be pitied; he cannot be dangerous. And a loyal subject of a Florentine prince can be something else: a patriot. What could be more proper for a Florentine than to call on the representative of the greatest family of his city to take the lead in the enterprise of liberating Italy?[2]

Machiavelli promises that his book will enable Lorenzo to understand in a short time what he, Machiavelli, has come to know and to understand. The whole of his knowledge and understanding is to be made available to the prince, and he need not suffer the hardships and dangers that Machiavelli has suffered. What of other readers? Do we therefore need no other work to discover the whole of the Machiavellian teaching? Machiavelli does not promise to present his whole teaching; rather, he promises to give the prince the faculty whereby he might be able to understand the whole of Machiavelli's teaching. We have to wonder how he proposes to do this. We shall rely on Machiavelli's promise and, as he suggests, with care diligently read and consider it.

NOTES

1. As he says in chapter XV, it is his "intention to write a useful thing for the one who understands."

2. Would that not mean that he would also be calling on the papacy to take the lead in liberating Italy? In *The Prince,* see chapter XI and his hope for His Holiness, Pope Leo X, and chapter XXVI.

PART ONE

OF PRINCIPATES

CHAPTER I

HOW MANY KINDS OF PRINCIPATES THERE ARE AND BY WHAT MODES THEY ARE ACQUIRED

The title of the work is *De Principatibus,* which reminds us of the Roman principate. Augustus Caesar refused the title of dictator, which Julius Caesar had adopted, preferring instead the title of *princeps,* with its strong republican associations. The *princeps senatus* was a title designating the senior member of the senate, whose name appeared first in the roll of members and who had the right to speak first. The significance of the title is that Augustus wished to preserve republican form.[1] What he established was not a *dominatio* but a *principatus,* hence a principate. In translating *principatus* as "principality," do we tend to lose this allusion? Does it tend to make the reader think not of the Roman principate but of the feudal principalities and of what is usually understood in Christian times as monarchical government? That is, one wonders whether Machiavelli's principate is meant to be more republican, if only in terms of associations evoked in the memory.

Furthermore, are we to think of the *princeps* as simply the "first man," or the highest kind of human being? Is that not the fundamental question at issue? What or who is the highest kind of human being?

. . .

The first sentence in Machiavelli's first chapter is what one would expect from a theoretical work on constitutions or regimes. It reminds one in its succinctness and universality of the opening of Aristotle's *Politics:* "All the states and all the dominions," he says, "that have had and have imperium[2] over men, have been and are either republics or principates." The imperium was the jurisdiction given a Roman magistrate within which he was to interpret and to execute the law, that is, to exercise the supreme executive power, which, of course, especially meant power over life and death. States and dominions, republics or principates, seem to be the entities through which such power over human beings can be exercised. Are we to understand that whatever has imperium over men is either a state or a dominion?[3]

We discover later, in chapter XV, that Machiavelli speaks of imaginary republics and princes. Are these able to exercise imperium over human beings, or are they simply ineffectual? And if imaginary republics and principates do have imperium, how is it obtained and exercised? We have noted that he does not mention ecclesiastical principates in this first list of topics that appear to be completely ineffectual yet are powerful and maintained by ancient orders and thus seem to have imperium. Are these to be distinguished from imagined principates?

Machiavelli also speaks of "principates of which we have memory" (IV.25), implying that there have been principates (and republics) of which we have no memory.

Does Machiavelli include forgotten states and dominions in his all-inclusive sentence? Perhaps he does, which would mean that we can know what such principates are like. We can infer from what we know of human nature what the principates, of which we have only the memory, must have been like. That would further signify that one rules human beings now as they have been ruled and will be ruled, for what is known about political rule is sempiternal and universal.

The first consequence of dividing all regimes in two, republics or principates, is that one no longer distinguishes between princes and tyrants.[4] (Machiavelli later makes a distinction between criminal and civil founders.) Machiavelli, of course, is himself speaking to a tyrant, and one must necessarily be silent about certain matters when addressing a tyrant, especially when one desires to obtain something from him. Moreover, to gain the tyrant's attention one must promise to give him something. In the Epistle Dedicatory Machiavelli has already shown us how tyrants are to be approached. It must, however, be asked whether a decent man, for the reasons given above, should ever speak with a tyrant. Socrates, for example, never speaks to a tyrant. Aristotle, in contrast, addresses tyrants in the *Politics,* showing them how they may preserve themselves. The usual justification for one's speaking with a tyrant is that one may be able to moderate his rule, and Aristotle's advice to tyrants has this end in view. The question, then, is whether Machiavelli also has a similar end. Indeed, does he not make us, his readers, consent to wickedness when we permit him not to distinguish between legitimate princes and tyrants and when he identifies virtue with acquiring with one's own arms? Thus if one successfully takes power with one's own arms and maintains oneself, one is virtuous; or, to be a successful tyrant is to be virtuous. Machiavelli not only removes all taint from tyranny but also overturns the moral order as traditionally understood, declaring that what is regarded as vicious is in fact virtuous.

At the beginning we have no indication of to whom the book is addressed, other than to Lorenzo de' Medici. Who, then, will benefit from the book? If Machiavelli is not addressing Lorenzo—and we have already argued that he is not—then he is not addressing someone who has obtained rule by means of fortune and the arms of others. Could he be addressing someone who has obtained rule by his own arms and virtue? Two other alternatives remain: a ruler who wishes to acquire provinces other than his own and one who lacks nothing for ruling but a kingdom. We know from the Epistle Dedicatory that Machiavelli holds most dear and esteems most the knowledge of the actions of great men. Must we not conclude that it is the one who knows and understands who deserves a kingdom? But what if fortune has not given such a one a kingdom? Would he not be the one who would find Machiavelli's work most useful? Would one who is already ruling because of his virtue already know what needs to be done? Thus the one who merits being a ruler and not one who is would be the proper addressee of the book. In other words, is Machiavelli not addressing potential rulers, which is to say, potential tyrants?

In Plato's *Republic,* two spirited young men ask Socrates, in effect, why they ought not be tyrants. The rest of the dialogue is Socrates's attempt to persuade especially Glaucon that there is a speech that defends and saves justice. In the painting *The School of Athens* Raphael depicts Socrates arguing with Alcibiades and Alexander the Great, two of the greatest tyrannical natures, the one prevented by circumstances from succeeding in his desire to rule the whole of the Mediterranean, the other the greatest Hellenistic conqueror. It is tempting to believe that Socrates is shown trying to persuade Alcibiades and Alexander away from their tyrannical desires—and there do exist two Platonic dialogues, the *Alcibiades* I and II, in which Socrates attempts to persuade Alcibiades from tyranny. Is it not of consequence whether young men such as these are turned from politics to philosophy by Socratic charm and wisdom? (That Socrates must have succeeded with Glaucon is perhaps shown by the fact that we hear no more of him.) One may ask why Socrates would wish to turn such young men away from the political life and why Machiavelli would seem to wish to do the opposite. Far from dissuading the spirited from tyranny, the opening chapter of *The Prince* would surely only encourage them to believe that it is virtue itself to indulge their desire to rule.

. . .

The examples of wholly new and mixed principates that Machiavelli cites are drawn from contemporary Italian experience. The first is of a native Italian mercenary captain, Sforza, who overthrew a republic and betrayed those who had hired him. The second is that of a foreigner who added a large part of Italy to his kingdom. Are these the two examples we are to keep in mind of how Italy is to be conquered? These examples, it should not escape our notice, are of the acquisition of northern and southern Italy.[5] What of central Italy, a region that includes Tuscany and Rome? And can Italy provide all the examples we need concerning the nature of regimes and how they are to be acquired?

NOTES

1. Edward Gibbon put it more strongly: the title *dominus,* he wrote, was "rejected with abhorrence by the first Caesars" (*The Decline and Fall of the Roman Empire* [New York: Modern Library, n.d.], I: 330–31; see also I: 57). The Roman principate is usually said to have lasted from Augustus to Diocletian. With Diocletian the period of the empire proper began, when the sovereign adopted the epithets *imperator* and *dominus et deus.*

2. The term *imperium* is preferable to *empire* because it is more precise and not misleading.

3. See the introduction to the Waveland edition of my translation of *The Prince* on Machiavelli's understanding of the state.

4. Aristotle distinguishes six regimes, three good and three bad. Machiavelli's radical simplification leaves no room for such distinctions.

5. Compare with Shakespeare's *Tempest,* where the marriage between Miranda and Ferdinand would unite northern and southern Italy.

CHAPTER II

OF HEREDITARY PRINCIPATES

The discussion of republics is omitted, as one can reasonably expect in a treatise on principates, especially because the topic was discussed elsewhere. Machiavelli will dispute the question of the principate—*The Prince* is a disputation, a formal debate on a thesis. (In chapter XV he acknowledges that his thesis is a most controversial one, for, he says, he departs "from the orders of others in the disputation of this matter.") He proposes to weave his argument "according to the order written above," that is, in chapter I. He promises to stay with the order of the written text,[1] but we have already noted his apparent departures from that order.

A hereditary state is one in which the blood of the prince is ancient. The first use of *sangue* (blood) is connected with the ancestral, the customary and habitual. Is attachment to the blood one of the first meanings of what is natural? The natural prince is one whose lineage or blood has long been accepted by the people.[2] What is habitually accepted can be called natural, for it is so much a part of things that one does not think that it could be otherwise.[3] We begin with what a natural prince is; the beginning, like that of the Epistle Dedicatory, is with the usual or the customary.

Machiavelli's first mention of nature, however, was in the context of understanding the nature of places, high and low, and therefore of princes and of the people. He appears to establish an analogy between knowledge of the natures of nonhuman things and of human things. How are these distinguished one from another, and how are they related? Is knowledge of the nature of nonhuman things the same as that of human things? What is the relationship between the natural as universal and sempiternal and the natural as ancestral or customary?

The natural or hereditary prince need only follow the order or regime established by his ancestors. He should follow constitutional usages; he has his throne by custom and should therefore not disturb customary or ancestral orders. Accidents, however, do occur, and here Machiavelli suggests that "ordinary industry" on the part of the prince is what is required. No extraordinary measures need be undertaken; presumably, such measures are to be contrasted with the unnatural or unusual, or the noncustomary. Indeed, temporizing with accidents would seem to be the best policy. To temporize is to allow an accident to have its way: one does not resort to extreme measures in attempting to correct it.

The advantage of a natural prince is, then, that he need not resort to extraordinary measures; he need have only "ordinary industry" to keep his state. At the end of the chapter Machiavelli advises the prince not to become hated because of extraordinary vices. He may have ordinary vices, as he is to have ordinary industry. One wonders, of course, what "extraordinary vices" means.

If the natural prince is deprived of his state and made a *privato* (private man), he may "reacquire" his state when the usurper meets with some mishap or accident.

The usurper seems more vulnerable to accident. The example given of how a natural prince is less vulnerable to attack is that of the duke of Ferrara, who, by being "ancient in that dominion," was able to withstand the attacks of the Venetians and the pope. The example is ambiguous because the incidents Machiavelli mentions occurred in the reigns of two different dukes of Ferrara. Ercole d'Este did stand up to the attack of Pope Sixtus IV in 1482, but Pope Julius II succeeded in driving out Alfonso d'Este in 1510. The latter, therefore, did not stand up to the pope. We should not, perhaps, be surprised that the first mention of the pope is as a usurper, against whom the natural prince has to defend himself.

A prince may be ordinary, in industry and vices alike, because the continuity of his dominion or mastery extinguishes memories and causes for innovations. He may thus make changes quietly and regularly. Are changes (*mutazioni*) to be distinguished from innovations (*innovazioni*)? The unnatural prince, we may conclude, is he who has introduced innovations, depriving the natural prince of the orders of his ancestors. Innovations may, however, be introduced by the hereditary prince without their appearing to be such. It would thus seem that the greatest accident to a natural prince would be his having to introduce innovations or, perhaps, his making it apparent that the changes that inevitably have to be made are in fact innovations. The counsel to temporize when accidents occur would be to try to show that the need for innovation does not exist. If the natural prince is able to do this, then the causes for innovation are not so much extinguished as they are hidden. Is it the task of the prince to become "natural," such that the causes for innovations appear to be extinguished?

NOTES

1. The written text establishes the order.
2. He speaks of the natural prince only in this chapter.
3. See Jacob Klein, "On the Nature of Nature," in *Lectures and Essays,* edited by Robert B. Williamson and Elliott Zuckerman (Annapolis, Md.: St. John's College Press, 1985), 220–21.

CHAPTER III
OF MIXED PRINCIPATES

Machiavelli now turns to his true matter, the establishment of new principates. He first, however, takes up those principates that are not wholly new rather than, as we might have expected from chapter I, those that are wholly new. He begins, as it were, not with Sforza but with the king of Aragon. The beginning is the desire to acquire that which belongs to another. The question that immediately arises is whether any acquisition can be wholly new. Must not every acquisition always belong to someone else first?

We are immediately told that it is the habit of men "willingly to change masters." Does this statement not cast fundamental doubt on what was said in the previous chapter about the stability of hereditary principates? Is there not always, therefore, a desire to innovate? Human beings, it would seem, always believe that their condition may be bettered, and this belief or faith (*credenza*) will always lead to dissatisfaction with the existing order. They are, of course, deceived in such a belief, but it arises from a natural desire that is a natural difficulty for the prince.

Suddenly Machiavelli addresses the prince in the intimate and equalizing second-person-singular *tu* form of address. Perhaps he did not expect his princely reader to go beyond the Epistle Dedicatory, if the latter opened it at all. In a very short time Machiavelli has come far from the low place he first occupied. Is he now on the heights with the prince, or are they both in the valley? Of course, the prince he so addresses is one who wishes to acquire. Is he not still, nonetheless, a prince? Is he also a natural prince about to become a new prince by conquering a province different from his own?

To enter into a province, Machiavelli says, "you" (*tu*) must have the favor of the provincials. One must have friends within the province. The king of France had such friends, but these, discovering that they had been deceived in this hope of a "future good," rebelled, and Milan had to be taken a second time. And now the French could not be driven from Italy until "the whole world" came against them. France tried twice to take Italy: the first attempt failed because the promise of the future did not come to pass. Does the liberation of Italy require that the "whole world" be invoked against those who presently occupy that province?

The beginning of Machiavelli's inquiry is the invasion of Italy by the king of France—the first example of acquisition that is discussed. Machiavelli calls what he is doing a discussion of causes. The inquiry is into the causes of successful and unsuccessful acquisition, of gain and loss. To understand these causes, he begins with the acquisition of that which belongs to others. The understanding of these causes leads to the possibility of remedies, and one may learn from the invasion of Italy what one ought or ought not do in acquiring states in a different province. Once one knows how to acquire Italy, presumably one will know how to acquire what is not one's own. Will one also learn how to defend what is one's own?

. . .

To understand the causes of gain and of loss in the attempt to acquire, Machiavelli turns to an examination of the province. The first question is whether a province is like one's own or is different. If the former, the prince can keep it with great ease, especially if its inhabitants are not used to a free life. Only two things need to be done: the line of the prince must be extinguished (he avoids the term *blood*) and the ancient customs kept. Supposedly, provinces that are like one's own may very soon become "all one body with the ancient principate"; provinces that are different from one's own can also be incorporated, but with difficulty and over a longer period of time. Is the difference in conquering such provinces really so great, or does it merely take longer?

He suggests that the principal remedy for the difficulty of holding a province different from one's own is that the conquering prince should go there to live. The example given is that of the Turk coming to live in Greece—a second instance of the conquest of a different province. As France passed into Italy, so did the Turk come over into Greece. Unlike the king of France, however, the Turk was successful in his conquest.

Machiavelli then gives the key example of how an outside power acquires a different province. The conquest of Greece by the Romans, however, was not by a prince but by a people; and it was kept by means of colonies, not by the prince's going there to live. Both are called "best" remedies for keeping a province whose acquisition was in effect the coming of strangers to dwell in a different land and making it their own. What happens to the conqueror and the conquered? Does the coming of a people, with their colonies, change a province more fundamentally than does the coming of a prince? And is it merely the conquered province that is changed, or does the conqueror also change? Would not both be fundamentally changed?

The example of the Romans, who were brought into Greece by the Aetolians, is the first ancient case cited by Machiavelli. His previous examples have been Italian, with the exception of the Turk in Greece, and all are modern. The example of Greece, says Machiavelli, is one he wishes would suffice as the only example of this point, that is, of what a powerful foreigner in a different province should do. The Romans are here the foreigners, and what they did to acquire Greece may also be done to acquire Italy. In listing the errors that Louis committed in his attempt to conquer Italy, Machiavelli makes it clear that Louis's strategy should have been that of the Romans. We learn from the Romans how a foreign power can conquer Italy. It is as Romans that we are to invade Italy; the Romans, we suddenly realize, are here to be regarded as foreign invaders.

To the rule of either going to live in a province or sending colonists, Machiavelli adds two additional rules that ought to be followed by one who is in a different province. The first is that one should become the head and defender of the weaker powers and therefore should contrive to weaken the powers of that province. The weak are to be patronized or encouraged. (The Italian is *intratenere* [entertain, in the archaic sense of maintaining or providing for].) Will this not make a province ill? What is strong in it (by nature?) is to be weakened, and it will certainly no longer be what it was. (Do provinces have a nature, and is it good, bad, or a matter of indifference if their natures are changed?)

The second additional rule is that one should beware of a more powerful foreigner entering the province by some accident, for the "order of things" is such that the weaker people will always, because of envy, attach themselves to a powerful foreigner, willingly making a "globe" with his state. The weak are always ready to turn to an outside power with whom they believe they can make a new "globe" or whole or world. We are told at the beginning of the chapter that "men willingly change masters," and we now see that this "natural difficulty" arises from the envy of the weak for those who have power over them.

The Romans are said to have knowledge of the things of the state, and the analogy used for such knowledge is that of medicine. Has such knowledge been transmitted to the moderns? The Romans used power intelligently; one notes the insistent repetition of the word *power* in the sentence that introduces the Romans: "The Romans, in the provinces they took, observed well these matters: they sent colonies, kept and provided for the less powerful without increasing their power, put down the powers, and never let powerful foreigners gain a reputation." We are left with no doubt that the Romans possessed knowledge of the use of power, and to have such knowledge is to have a remedy, a medicine, for political ills or maladies. Knowledge and power are here mentioned together; they seem to be closely connected to one another. The enterprise of Italy seems ultimately to be the enterprise of knowledge itself.

. . .

From the ancient example we return to the contemporary example of the king of France. As he enters this part of the discussion, Machiavelli addresses a "you," but this "you" is not the intimate *tu* of the beginning of the chapter but a courteous, third-person-singular *voi*. Whoever this *voi* is, he is always asked to see, to consider, or to think. The one addressed as *tu* is, we recall, the one who wishes to acquire, who is an agent or an actor.

The principal obstacle to the conquest of Italy by France is the "greatness" of the church. Strikingly, Machiavelli avoids speaking of the power of the church. Greatness and power are to be distinguished from each other. Greatness implies glory; that is, a showing or manifestation. Lorenzo, we remember from the Epistle Dedicatory, is promised greatness by his fortune. In the first chapter fortune and virtue are to be contrasted. To depend on the arms of others is to depend on fortune; to depend on one's own arms is self-sufficiency and virtue. Thus virtue and power are to be connected one with another, but to rely on fortune is to be weak. Greatness may be attained by those who lack virtue and power; but does the possession of virtue and power imply greatness, or can these be unadorned, lack showiness, ostentation, or magnificence, and therefore lack greatness?

To say that the greatness of the church is the principal obstacle to the conquest of Italy leads us to wonder how the church came to such greatness. We cannot help but be reminded of the conquest of the Roman Empire by the Church of Rome. Two Romes exist, but one apparently had power and the other has greatness. What accounts for the difference, and why is the greatness of the second Rome such an obstacle to the conquest of Italy? We now see that Roman modes of conquering a foreign province are to be used in conquering an Italy in which the principal obstacle is the church. The Romans, it would seem, are to recapture Rome. The end of the chapter reminds us of the difference between the Romans of the republic and those of present-day Italy. Present-day Italy, as the cardinal of Rouen says to Machiavelli, seems to have lost the knowledge of war that the ancient Romans had. What has happened to the Roman republic and to modern Italy?

To desire to acquire is now said to be natural and ordinary. The Epistle Dedicatory already suggested that the desire to acquire makes human beings equal. It is the natural and ordinary condition of men, both high and low. It is a necessity that excuses the actions of a prince and, it would seem, of human beings in general. We are also reminded of the natural prince of chapter II, who is to be ordinary in his policies and his vices. Would not being ordinary mean that he will desire to acquire and will himself be an object of acquisition? Put together with the other natural desire mentioned, that of men to change masters, will he not always be threatened by some "accident"? Could one meaning of a natural prince be that he is one who does not go beyond the expected orders of things or go beyond that which is given by nature? To be a natural prince is to use ordinary, and not extraordinary, modes. Perhaps to be "of the blood" refers to being human, nothing more, that is, to be an inheritor or son of humanity with all the frailties of the flesh.

Machiavelli claims to know the nature of princes, the actions of great men. We now see that the greatest actions arise from a natural and ordinary desire. Acquisition is the natural and ordinary activity of human beings, but it is the prince who must know how to acquire, especially a foreign province or a province different from his own. To acquire such a province requires great fortune and great industry, for the difficulties are infinite. Thus the ordinary and natural desire of human beings leads to enterprises of the utmost difficulty. Could not one say that it leads to the greatest and perhaps highest of human activities, which is still, nonetheless, natural and ordinary? Machiavelli will soon speak of Alexander the Great and his enterprises.

. . .

Toward the end of the chapter, we are told that the greatest error Louis XII committed was that of taking away the state from the Venetians in Italy. In so doing, he destroyed the only ally he had against the church and Spain. What is subsequently discussed, however, is not the destruction of the power of the Venetians but the second and third errors in the list of the five errors Louis committed: those of increasing the power of a powerful one and of bringing an extremely powerful foreigner into Italy.

Machiavelli speaks of someone who puts forward the argument that King Louis strengthened the church and Spain in Italy because he wanted to avoid war. Machiavelli responds, as if to a scholastic disputation, citing the reasons "above" that explain why the Romans never avoided war. If Roman reasons had been followed, presumably the church would never have come to greatness in Italy. Would a foreigner also have been prevented entry?

A second argument alleged by some others, according to Machiavelli, is that the error regarding the church (again, not Venice) was caused by the obligation the king incurred for the pope's resolution of his marriage and the elevation of the archbishop of Rouen to the College of Cardinals. Machiavelli tells these others to go "below" to see what he says about the faith of princes. The first paragraph of chapter XVIII, which appears to be the chapter in question, states that "princes who have done great things have taken little account of faith." The king should not have kept his faith or his pledge to the pope, especially because Alexander VI was himself the greatest breaker of oaths or faith.

The faith pledged by the king is caused by his desire to annul his marriage. One is made to reflect on the point that one of the causes of the church's greatness may well be its power to legitimize the blood, that is, the lineage of the prince or the succession.[1] Is there a connection between the church and the blood, in the sense of the customary and the ancestral? Are the church and what it represents that which make a prince "natural" in the sense of chapter II? The importance of the church in temporal affairs may be indicated by the desire for a cardinal's hat; temporal rulers seek representation in the hierarchy of the church.

One cannot escape the thought that the someone and the others who may defend King Louis do so in terms especially reminiscent of Christian doctrine: the avoidance of war and the keeping of faith. We have seen how the Romans viewed the first policy, and we shall have to wait to see fully what Machiavelli says about keeping faith. We are now told that the failure of King Louis was not a miracle but ordinary and reasonable. It is this ordinary and reasonable matter of which Machiavelli speaks to the cardinal of Rouen himself. Machiavelli's response in this discussion takes on a special pungency, for what he says to a prince of the church, one who had led his king to ruin,[2] is that the French did not understand the things of the state and therefore allowed the church to come to greatness in Italy.

We recall again that Machiavelli cited Roman "reasons" in his first response. Did the Romans understood statecraft in a way that the French did not? The point should be emphasized: to know the things of the state is to know that one should not let the church come to greatness.

We are finally given a Machiavellian rule or precept, one that, we are promised, "never or rarely fails." The rule is "that he who is cause of another's becoming powerful ruins himself." Machiavelli promises to teach the prince who wishes to acquire how to do so successfully; how can he be the cause of a prince's becoming powerful without himself becoming suspect?

The rule Machiavelli puts forward, as well as the previous claim he makes for the statecraft of the Italians, raises the question of his own status. How does his knowledge of the things of the state compare with that of the ancients? The Romans possessed both the political and martial arts, for they were able to foresee difficulties from afar, and such foresight is given only to those who are prudent; and to be prudent is to know the things of the state. The ancients had an undivided knowledge that the moderns do not have. Does Machiavelli also know the things of war?

Machiavelli speaks in his own name at the end of this chapter (indeed, he responds three times in his own name in the immediately preceding passage), and he gives a rule that is apparently his own. Is his knowledge Roman, or is it his own?

Moreover, one cannot avoid noticing that the rule Machiavelli puts forward conceals a blasphemous thought. Is it not the fundamental biblical teaching that God is the cause of one's becoming powerful?

. . .

The enterprise or conquest of Italy is the beginning of inquiry into the causes of successful and unsuccessful acquisition. We see that it is an inquiry into the natural and ordinary activity of human beings, into the causes of this human activity of acquisition and the remedies human beings have. At the end of the chapter we begin to see the significance of the lack of knowledge, a knowledge that comprises both war and the state.

NOTES

1. Shakespeare's English history plays provide an excellent illustration of the importance of legitimizing the line of succession. One need only think, of course, of what happened in the reign of Henry VIII of England.

2. Georges d'Amboise, the cardinal of Rouen, was also prime minister to King Louis XII.

CHAPTER IV

WHY THE KINGDOM OF DARIUS WHICH ALEXANDER HAD SEIZED DID NOT REBEL AGAINST HIS SUCCESSORS AFTER THE DEATH OF ALEXANDER

The title of this chapter is the only one that contains the names of persons. Proper names are in the titles of only three chapters, IV, XXIV, and XXVI, with the latter two naming Italy. Alexander is named in this title twice; one must certainly wonder about the repetition.[1] The title of chapter XXIV also speaks of the loss of a kingdom: the kingdom of Darius is lost, and so is that of the princes of Italy. Furthermore, this chapter title is the only one in which death is mentioned, the death of one of the greatest conquerors. The title explicitly raises the question of what continues after death.[2] In the case of Alexander's conquest of Asia, the cause is to be found in the "subject," that is, in the province in question.

Machiavelli begins the discussion with a distinction between two modes of governing principates. He has not prepared us for this distinction, and we are now told of a kind of principate that looks as though it is a mean between liberty and despotism. The examples of the two modes are the Turk and the king of France. According to the title of the chapter, we are to learn why Alexander and his successors were able to hold the kingdom of Darius. The Turk, we recall, has successfully kept Greece, whereas France has lost Italy. We are to learn now how to conquer Asia, not Italy.

The difference between the two modes of government is that in one the prince governs absolutely and all his ministers are his servants, and in the other, which appears to be a description of the feudal order, the barons have their own states and subjects and hold their rank "not by the grace of the lord, but by the antiquity of their blood." These barons have their own loyal and loving subjects; they have privileges that the lord cannot take away without danger to himself. We may say simply that in one kind of province there are many lords with their own jurisdictions, while in another there is but one lord to whom all are in servitude. This has been said to be the precise difference between the gentile religions and the biblical.[3]

The state of the Turk is therefore difficult to acquire, but once acquired it is easy to hold, for there are no barons to challenge one's rule. The state of France is easy to acquire, for one can always enter because of a discontented baron; it is, however, difficult to hold, for these lords will always be disappointed in their expectations.[4] The conquest by France of provinces that are similar in customs must have necessitated the extinction of the blood of their ancient princes. (Machiavelli now speaks of the blood of the prince, not of his line.) It could not have been as easy as we were led to believe in chapter III. On the contrary, because it is easier to extinguish the blood of an absolute prince it is easier to acquire his state.

Machiavelli asks his reader to consider the nature of Darius's government, and it is the first request he has made of this "you" whom he addresses courteously. The government is similar to that of the Turk. It appears that the province of Asia produces the same kind of government, whether it is held by Darius or by the Turk. Like France, Gaul has many lords.[5]

To conquer a province one must know its nature, and we now see that this nature is like the nature of nonhuman things. The nature of the province persists through millennia, for Turkey is the same as Persia and France is the same as Gaul. We repeat a question first raised when discussing the Epistle Dedicatory: does Machiavelli distinguish between knowledge of the nature of nonhuman things and of human things? Or is the knowledge that permits us to conquer as Alexander conquered a knowledge of the natures of all things? If chapter III launched us on the enterprise of Italy, we are now to compare it in chapter IV with the Alexandrian enterprise of Asia. We see that the different natures of the provinces, which can seemingly be as enduring as the topography of the land itself, require different modes or strategies of acquisition.

If we remember that Darius III is the last of the line of Achaemenids, we realize that Darius's government was one established by Cyrus. The reader is asked to consider the nature of Cyrus's government: as we know from, among others, Herodotus, Xenophon, and the Bible, that government was one which showed how to rule human beings and, indeed, claimed to rule all mankind.[6] The kingdom of Darius or Cyrus is therefore the kingdom that claims dominion over all of mankind.

The government of Darius is like that of the Turk: the absolute rule of the herdsman over his herd. We may therefore interpret the title of this chapter as considering, "Why the kingdom of all human beings which Alexander had occupied did not rebel against his successors after the death of Alexander." That is to say, one may marvel or wonder that the rule of one who claimed and took the kingdom of all human beings somehow persisted despite his early death and despite quarrels among his successors.

May not, however, the nature of a province be changed? The Romans are said to have been able finally "to extinguish" the memory of the principates in the provinces they had conquered. We now realize that the Romans had changed the nature of their provinces, such that they became like Turkey or like Asia. Is this why Italy has lost the art of warfare? The first example given of acquisition was the invasion or conquest of Italy as a foreign nation. The counsel given was that Roman rules or Roman modes should be followed in order to conquer Italy as one would conquer a province different from one's own. The enterprise of Italy has now become the enterprise of Cyrus's kingdom. We learn how to conquer the kingdom that claims dominion over all human beings in such a way that it will not rebel against the successors of whoever conquers it. The question, of course, is the relationship between these two enterprises. We begin to see the full extent of Machiavelli's enterprise.

We are left with the thought that Pyrrhus and "many others" have failed to conquer provinces, not because of their greater or lesser virtue but because of—one is tempted to say because of the nature of—the province in question. Pyrrhus, king of Epirus, who allied himself with one of Alexander's successors, failed to conquer Italy. Are we to contrast this failure with the success of the Hellenistic rulers in Asia?

NOTES

1. Xenophon's name also appears twice at the end of chapter XIV.

2. The first and last words of *The Prince* are "[They are] usually . . . dead" (*Sogliono . . . morto*).

3. See Leo Strauss, *Thoughts on Machiavelli* (Glencoe, Ill.: Free Press, 1958), 49, 188.

4. See the beginning of chapter III above.

5. That Machiavelli knows that the name "France" is anachronistic is shown in the *Discourses* III.43. The chapter is entitled "That Men Who Are Born in a Province Keep for All Times Almost the Same Nature."

6. Herodotus, *History* VII.8; Xenophon, *Cyropaedia* I.i.1–6; II Chronicles 36:22–23; Ezra 1:1–4. See also Josephus, *Antiquities* XI.i.1 ff.: "For he [God] stirred up the spirit [*psychin*] of Cyrus and caused him to write throughout all Asia, 'Thus says King Cyrus. Since the Most High God has appointed me king of the habitable world [*oikoumenis*], I am persuaded that He is the god whom the Israelite nation worships, for He foretold my name through the prophets and that I should build His temple in Jerusalem in the land of Judaea.'"

CHAPTER V

IN WHAT MODE CITIES OR PRINCIPATES MUST BE ADMINISTERED WHICH BEFORE THEY WERE SEIZED USED TO LIVE BY THEIR OWN LAWS

Cities that lose their liberty, as the title tells us, are now to be administered, for they no longer govern themselves. We have just considered the differences between acquiring France and the kingdom of Darius, and we are now to consider the acquisition of cities that live by their own laws and in liberty or the acquisition of republics. Republics are usually cities: the shapelessness of an empire and the too-great spiritedness of a tribe prevent the possibility of a republic. The acquisition of a city, as we shall see, presents a greater difficulty than that of a principate with barons.

Machiavelli presents three modes of keeping such states but discusses only two, the extremes. Cities must either be permitted to live under their own laws or be wholly destroyed. To let them live under their own laws, the prince should create a state of a few or an oligarchy dependent on him, which keeps it friendly to him. The example of such a mode is Sparta. The Spartans were generous, freeing the cities under them and "leaving them to their own laws," and they lost Greece. The Romans wished to follow the Spartan example, but they were finally forced to destroy many cities in Greece, dispersing the inhabitants entirely. The kindly intentions of the Romans succumb to the demands of necessity. Republics must be utterly destroyed when conquered, or else they will destroy the conquerors.

To rule by laws is to rule according to that which is proper to man,[1] and to rule by force is to rule according to the beasts. The Spartans, we may say, tried to rule the Greek cities "humanly" or humanely; Roman rule, of necessity, is a "beastly" rule, a cruel rule. Sparta thus is the apparently failed attempt to rule according to reason, whereas Roman rule is the denial of the rule of reason in political or human things. To choose the Romans is to choose the rule of necessity or the beast. We also see what happened to Greece after it was conquered by the Romans; its cities and liberties were destroyed.

The only sure mode of holding republics is to destroy them, because those who have lived in liberty and under their own laws never forget their ancient orders, and neither length of time nor benefits suffices to make them forget. In other words, the citizens of republics, such as Athens and Thebes, behave like "great personages" or aristocrats who never forget past injuries.[2] The last sentence of the chapter seems to have passion behind it, and it could be the warning of a patriot to a tyrant: "But in republics there is greater life, greater hate, more desire for vengeance; the memory of ancient liberty does not leave them, nor can it let them rest." Would the long duration of the Roman Empire suffice to destroy such memories? Or are we now to reconsider the concluding remarks of chapter IV? Will the memory of ancient liber-

ties ever be extinguished in Greece, or will the name of liberty and therefore its orders never be forgotten? That is, would it be possible for its name to be remem-
bered later? The tone of the chapter makes us believe that the ancient orders of liberty will never be forgotten and that the tyranny of such people as the Romans will
one day be overthrown by those whose city has been occupied.

The harsh and extreme teaching, that republics must be destroyed, ought not distract us from what is the most significant teaching of the chapter: that the ancient
orders of liberty were destroyed by the Romans but are never forgotten. Not all of
Greece was destroyed, although "many cities" were.[3] Is this chapter, then, a reassurance that the memory of liberty will not disappear? If the inhabitants of the fatherland are not disunited or dispersed, they will attempt to restore it. Those who
have always lived under a prince—as have, for example, the subjects of the kingdom of Darius—will be unable in the first place to agree on a successor once "the
blood" of their prince has been extinguished; they will not know how to defend
themselves, and they will forget their former orders. The name of liberty is more
persistent than the blood of a prince.

The modern example given of the persistence of the name of liberty is Pisa,
which, despite its century of servitude to the Florentines, rebelled when the occasion arose.[4] Pisa is also the principal example of the attempt to hold a city by means
of fortresses. Is servitude to the Florentines somehow to be thought of in connection with the servitude of Greece to the Turk? We simply note the juxtaposition, although it is difficult to construe the meaning. Florence, unlike Rome, is a weak, unarmed republic that relies on mercenaries, factions, and fortresses. Florence,
furthermore, is the republic in which one best sees the effects of the sins of Italy.
How is it, then, that Florence may be thought of in conjunction with the Turk?
Moreover, should we think too of the servitude of Machiavelli to the House of the
Medici? Finally, are we also somehow to consider the significance of the betrayal
of Fermo to Oliverotto? In other words, are the servitude of Machiavelli to the
Medici, of Pisa to Florence, of Fermo to Oliverotto, and of Greece to the infidels
somehow interconnected?

The last word of the chapter is *abitarvi* (live there), and it is the only allusion to
the second mode of rule over acquired cities. It is the literal middle mode, between
the extremes of the Spartans and the Romans. That middle, which Machiavelli does
not discuss at all, would be neither wholly human nor wholly of the beast; it would
be half human and half beast.

The middle way, then, is to come to live in the province that one has conquered.
It reminds us of what the Turk did: the Turk came to live in Greece; the Romans ruined Greece. Is a barbarian prince able to exercise more moderation than are the republican Romans?

One could interpret *abitarvi* as meaning that the prince should come to live in
the ancient orders of republics. Because there is greater hate and more desire for
vengeance in republics, the safest policy of the prince is either to extinguish liberty or to live there in liberty. Perhaps the province the Machiavellian prince

wishes to rule is the province that is the ancient orders of liberty.

Machiavelli seems to be leading us to the possibility of a prince who reacquires the orders of liberty but imitates not the Roman republicans but a prince of Asia, Cyrus—keeping in mind that the government of Darius is the same as that of the Turk. Is Machiavelli's mode of holding a republic neither Spartan nor Roman? If we have followed the clues correctly, then we are faced with the difficulty that, on the one hand, the Romans are to be contrasted to the Greeks and the moderns, for their modes are those neither of Sparta nor of Florence. On the other hand, the Romans are the destroyers of liberty; their modes of conquest are cruel and inhuman and therefore not the ones ultimately to be followed.

The enterprise of Italy leads to the conclusion that where modern barbarian, King Louis, and ancient Greek, Pyrrhus, have failed, Roman modes of conquest should have been used. In chapter III, Roman modes are exemplary, and almost the whole of chapter V is given to a consideration of them. But are Machiavelli's modes Roman? Is his mode that not of the extremes but of the true and neglected middle?

We may think of this chapter as the perfect illustration of the Machiavellian emphasis on the extremes, concealing the far more moderate teaching. He makes it seem as though the choice is between the humanity of the Spartans[5] and the cruelty of the Romans, apparently concluding with a bloodthirsty call for the extinction of a city—if one wishes to keep it. What is said offhandedly and in passing is the more humane remedy. Why does Machiavelli, unlike the ancients, deliberately conceal his moderation, leaving the impression that he advocates only the harshest and most indecent of teachings?

NOTES

1. See *The Prince* XVIII.107.

2. *The Prince* VII.48; compare IX.59.

3. Compare this with the discussion of chapter XXIV.

4. Machiavelli speaks four times of "servitude" (*servitù*): in the Epistle Dedicatory, where he offers himself in servitude; here in chapter V; in chapter VIII, where the Firmani love servitude more than the fatherland; and in chapter XIII, where he speaks of "the beginning of the servitude of Greece under the infidels."

5. It is strange, of course, that Machiavelli chooses the Spartans as the example of compassionate rule. Compare Plutarch, "Lysander," in the *Lives*.

CHAPTER VI

OF NEW PRINCIPATES WHICH BY ONE'S ARMS
AND VIRTUE ARE ACQUIRED

We are asked at the beginning not to marvel at what Machiavelli will do,[1] not to marvel if, as he writes, in the speech "I shall make" "I shall address the greatest examples." Yet those who have founded new states are all marvelous (*tutti mirabili*). Marvels are, of course, told of such men. Plutarch remarks on the myths and legends that surround Theseus and Romulus, making them fit subjects not so much of historians as of tragic poets and mythographers.

We note that these men are private men who become princes and therefore are not natural princes in the sense of chapter II. Are they not, however, princes by nature, in the sense of what they essentially are, of what they are born to be? They are the innovators or founders of new orders, and they are the most ancient examples yet cited. The first mention of founders or innovators is placed, perhaps safely for someone who is addressing a prince, in the most distant of times. We can only imitate such wonderful men; we follow an already traveled path. We cannot attain their height, but to the extent that we can, we must be like them. We are to be like prudent archers, aiming high in order to hit low. (Chiron the Centaur, we remind ourselves, was an archer.)

The chapter is concerned with the founding of new orders. Four founders are said to be most excellent because they became princes by their own virtue and not by fortune: Moses, Cyrus, Romulus, and Theseus. For the first time, the ambiguity in chapter I is cleared up—to acquire with one's own arms is to acquire by virtue; to acquire with the arms of others, we shall see in chapter VII, is to acquire by fortune.

Moses, Cyrus, Romulus, and Theseus founded kingdoms and not republics, but two of these orders, which happen also to be cities—Rome and Athens—did become republics. If Rome and Athens have something in common, perhaps Israel and Persia may also in some respect be the same. Such a suspicion is confirmed when the orders of Moses and Cyrus are said to be "not discrepant" with one another. We also recall from chapter IV that Italy and Greece are of the same character, to be distinguished from Persia.

A founding is necessarily a break with established orders; therefore, when Machiavelli says that such men have ennobled their fatherland, they have no fatherland. We realize that it is especially the founder of a new order who can follow the precept to live in his acquisition. Not to have a state elsewhere may, of course, have yet another meaning: to have a state somewhere other than in this world. If one had such a state, could he come to live in his new acquisition?

. . .

Machiavelli describes the occasion or matter that each of these men had. Thus Moses found the Israelites enslaved; Cyrus had the discontented Persians; Theseus brought together a people who had been scattered in villages. When we come, however, to the occasion or the matter that Romulus had, it is said to be that he was exposed at birth. Machiavelli declares that it was "necessary" for Moses to find the Israelites enslaved and "needful" that Cyrus find the Persians malcontent, but Theseus is said to have "found" the Athenians scattered, and it was "fitting" that Romulus be exposed at birth. There is clearly more matter for Moses and Cyrus than for Theseus, and Romulus appears hardly to have had any occasion whatsoever to make him happy. All except Romulus had good fortune, which is apparently the same as a happy circumstance, of which their virtue could then make use. No flaw in the body politic is mentioned, no oppressed minority or other situation that he might have exploited.

Machiavelli further qualifies his distinctions. The success of founders depends on virtue, fortune, and the happy circumstance of a lack of other states that forces a prince to live in his new domain. Fortune is not absent, then, from this discussion of the most excellent men. Machiavelli brushes the apparent contradiction aside with the remark that fortune provided nothing but the occasion; virtue is what enabled these men to make use of the occasion. But what does fortune do except provide an occasion?

. . .

Machiavelli wishes to call attention to the peculiarity of Romulus's circumstance, for in the lists of the great founders he consistently changes the sequence in which Romulus's name appears. In the first list it appears third, then second, and finally last. The name of Moses always appears first; Cyrus's name is second twice; and Theseus's name twice appears in last place. In chapter XXVI, when Machiavelli again refers to the founders, the name of Romulus is conspicuously missing. The absence of his name is particularly conspicuous because the chapter calls for the revival of ancient—that is, Roman—virtue, so that Italy may be liberated and, implicitly, a new Rome may be established. Is Machiavelli questioning the status of Romulus as a founder? It is as though we were to speak of the restoration of Israel without mentioning Moses. The silence about Romulus makes one wonder whether some other name should be substituted for his when one is thinking of the refounding of Rome. Or perhaps Machiavelli has reason for calling special attention to Romulus. Is he also indicating that an occasion need not be provided by fortune? Romulus seems to have had no occasion of which he could make use; that is, he made an occasion out of his humble birth.

It is, however, neither Romulus nor Theseus who is prominent in chapter VI. Instead, Machiavelli speaks principally of Moses and Cyrus. He declares at first that one ought not to expect "reason" of Moses, for he was simply an instrument of God. Moses' actions would thus be beyond the ordinary and reasonable, the consequence of causes that cannot be understood by the merely human mind. Moreover, because God was the original source of his actions, it would seem that Moses could not be placed among the most excellent and celebrated men whose principal characteristic was self-sufficiency. Moses, however, ought still to be admired and may therefore remain in this great company, for he was considered worthy to speak to God face-to-face.[2] God would then be the true innovator; Machiavelli wishes to be as literal as possible in his reading of the Bible. God, not Moses, is the founder of the orders of Israel. Extraordinary blasphemy has thus been committed: Moses is placed on the same level as any founder of any kingdom; he is not different from a Romulus or a Cyrus, and a choice is therefore placed before us. Either the kingdom of Israel is simply another earthly kingdom, or God is a founder who can be thought of as acting as any other founder has acted.

We are to turn then to Cyrus, of whom one can expect reason, as Xenophon has already demonstrated. We are left with no doubt that, of the excellent and celebrated men, it is Cyrus who is to be imitated. When we consider Cyrus, we find that his actions are not different from those of Moses. Moses' actions are as reasonable (and as wonderful) as those of Cyrus. What is commanded of Moses and what Cyrus does on his own are similar. God, after all, arouses Cyrus to rebuild the temple in Jerusalem; the difference is that Cyrus does not speak to God face-to-face. Machiavelli therefore makes a general conclusion that includes Moses: fortune provided these men only with the occasion; the virtue or strength of their *animo* is what made the occasion known to them so they could take advantage of it.

The term *animo* may be translated as mind or spirit. Machiavelli never uses the word for soul, *anima*, in *The Prince*, although he uses it elsewhere. Instead, therefore, of speaking of the virtue or the strength of their souls, which would seem to be natural here, he uses a more ambiguous word. Here it is the *animo* that is not only the source of the form or the orders the innovator wishes to introduce but also what makes the occasion known. It is the virtue of the *animo* that principally makes these men great, that is, the virtue of what appears to be a combination of knowledge and spiritedness. Fortune, in contrast, provides the occasion. To what extent, then, is fortune the arbiter of greatness? If one with a virtuous *animo* has no proper occasion, must he content himself with an obscure life? We have already heard of what the extreme and excessive malignity of fortune can do, especially when it is continuous.

Is there another great blasphemy here? Did fortune provide the occasion for Moses? Does Machiavelli mean to substitute fortune for God?

. . .

Machiavelli's distinction between form and matter permits us to understand the relationship between the state and the province. We have seen that a state may expand or decrease in a province and that several princes may have a state in a province. If the state is the form or order that a prince wishes to introduce into the matter of a province, then one may be more or less successful in doing so. Perhaps we should speak of the *animo* and the state in terms of the will. The type of state one has in a province determines how much one's will obtains in it. Thus one may also understand the province as the substratum or matter into which the form of the state—the construct of the mind and will of the founder—is to be introduced. In what way, then, is founding a province different from acquiring one? Was not the passage of the French into Italy the natural wish of Louis XII to introduce the form of his *animo* into Italy?

The well-known simile of the prudent archer and the bow makes clear that knowledge is in the service of power. Prudence or knowledge sees the extent of the capacities or virtues at one's disposal. Prudence then enables us to judge our strength or virtue of mind, and that virtue is the making or bringing-to-be of new orders.

. . .

Machiavelli returns to the question of whether these "innovators stand on their own or if they depend on others." He introduces a new distinction, that between armed prophets and unarmed ones. (He never uses the word "prophet" elsewhere, either in *The Prince* or in the *Discourses*.) Moses, Cyrus, Theseus, and Romulus are armed prophets. Are they prophets because the orders they desire to establish are from God? Such men are close to God, for if Moses was worthy of speaking face-to-face with God, then Cyrus was not different from him, and neither, we can assume, were Theseus and Romulus. Indeed, is not Machiavelli saying that whoever understands how to establish new orders has spoken with God? These are the ones whose faces are shining as they come down from Mount Sinai. Hence they are prophets, but armed ones, because to establish their orders they have to use force. The nature of the people is fickle, so they are apt to change; are not the people thus part of the matter that has to be shaped? The people and the matter are variable and require form.

The one unarmed prophet mentioned is Savonarola, the Dominican friar who attempted to make Florence a Christian republic. Perhaps an unarmed prophet is one who relies entirely on the virtue of his *animo*. The example, however, necessarily raises the question of the status of Christianity. Was not Savonarola imitating his Master, who is the exemplar of the unarmed prophet? Did not Christianity triumph over the ancient religions? The old confrontation between Christianity and ancient politics is suddenly before us: it is the theme of Augustine's *City of God*.[3] Is Machiavelli, after so many centuries, asking once again whether an unarmed theology can rule the people? The distinction between the armed prophet and the unarmed one is, in truth, one between a civil or armed theology and an unarmed, otherworldly one. An armed theology is one that defends itself against the fickleness of the people; it cannot hold firm against the unbelief of the people and is therefore dependent on them.

Augustine understood the issue well when he took it up in the *City of God*. The civil theology, he declares, was invented by the founders of cities in order to rule the people. It is a calculated deception, so that the princes might bind the people up "more firmly in civil society so that they might . . . possess them as subjects."[4] According to Augustine, the philosophers have willingly abetted this deception, the purpose of which is to moderate the natural envy the people have of the rich and the powerful.

Augustine is of the opinion that the princes and the great deceive the people, the weak and the ignorant, because it is in their interest to do so. They must keep the truth from the people that their rule is unjust and oppressive. The civil theology is simply the ideology of the ruling class, as Karl Marx would have called it. The people ought to know of such deceptions, for the strength to know the truth has been made available to all in and through the incarnation. The people need no longer be deceived, for a new order of things has now been established, one that gives to all men the possibility of being free. No moderation of human passions is necessary, for matter itself has been redeemed. According to Augustine, the ancients thought that the difference between good men and bad men is that the good regard empire as necessity and the bad regard empire as felicity, but Christians believe that empire is only a vicious lust for sovereignty and glory.

In speaking of the armed prophet, Machiavelli is reasserting the necessity of the civil theology, or the necessity of having to rule the unregenerate human being. The question he raises is, in effect, whether it is true that matter or the people have been redeemed or so changed that what was thought necessary to rule them is no longer needed. If acquisition is a natural and ordinary necessity, as we have been told in chapter III, then one must do all the difficult things described in chapters III through V that are generally regarded as oppressive and unjust. Only if acquisition is not a necessity can one condemn the attempt to clothe decently the origins of political rule.

The unarmed prophets have no way of dealing with the people or with necessity, so they are easily brought to ruin. And yet, we remember, somehow the nature of the province of Italy has been changed, such that Italians no longer know the things of war. Machiavelli has also spoken of the greatness of the church in Italy. Are we not to remember that Christianity did conquer the Romans and Rome? Perhaps, therefore, we cannot say that unarmed prophets always fail, but Machiavelli would surely argue that the necessities of the world remain ever the same. We are thus left for the moment to puzzle over the status of the unarmed prophet.

. . .

We have been led in this chapter to consider the most fundamental issue of all. In speaking of the greatest men and the greatest actions Machiavelli forces us to consider the choice as to the order that ought to govern human things. Which of the prophets are we to believe—the armed or the unarmed? Furthermore, we understand what Machiavelli means when he indicates that the political is what is ordinary and reasonable, and not miraculous, for the unarmed prophet relies on the miraculous.

Indeed, the purpose of chapter VI seems to be to make the great innovators, especially the greatest innovator of all, ordinary and reasonable. Perhaps that is what Machiavelli also meant when he said at the beginning of the chapter that one is not to marvel. Cyrus is as much a prophet as is Moses, and both are armed. To be armed is to be ordinary and reasonable or natural. Not to be armed would be unreasonable and unnatural, so it may be the unarmed prophet who truly wants to innovate by relying on the marvelous.

We are also reminded that these men have great difficulty conducting their enterprise. They are "conductors," and the past particle of *condurre, condotta,* is also the word

used for the contract with which the services of the *condottiere* were bought.[5] Is
this the first hint of the character of these private men who become princes through
their virtue?

. . .

At the end of the chapter, Machiavelli adds one more name to the list of four, a
"lesser example," but one that is "good" when taken in "proper proportion": Hiero of
Syracuse. In chapter XIII, after listing another set of four names, Machiavelli similarly adds a fifth, but one that is not said to be lesser. Are we to understand that four
names are all that are required but that one somehow needs to be added each time?

We shall understand why he adds a fifth name to each of these lists of four only
when we compare the two lists, a comparison we shall make in the proper place. In
the context of chapter VI, the addition of Hiero of Syracuse has the further effect of
making the four great innovators less marvelous. For there is no disproportion between a Hiero, on the one hand, and a Cyrus or Moses, on the other hand—they are
of the same kind.

At the end of chapter IV, Machiavelli remarks that the failure of "Pyrrhus and his
kind" was caused not by a lack of virtue in the conqueror but by the difference in
what was being conquered. The matter may prove impermeable to the form, that is,
to the *animo* of the conqueror. The question may, in other words, be one of fortune:
Pyrrhus is no different in kind from Alexander; what makes them different is the
occasion or the matter that fortune provides.

If such men are of the same kind, then the actions of a Hiero are the same as those
of the greatest examples. The knowledge of the actions of great men may be obtained
from an examination of the actions of a Hiero "and his kind." In chapter VII, Machiavelli examines the actions of Cesare Borgia. Must not Cesare be of the same kind as
Hiero? Hiero is a captain: it is the first time the title is used, and it signifies one who is
capable of commanding and who possesses the strategic art. If Hiero is a captain,
must we not also conclude that the other innovators are also captains?

. . .

Machiavelli's desire to add Hiero's name to the list in chapter VI permits him to
use a Latin quotation from an ancient historian. For the first time in *The Prince* he
cites an ancient writer as an authority. The Latin quotation declares that Hiero
"lacked nothing for ruling but a kingdom." That is, Hiero is one of those who
should rule by nature but has no kingdom to rule. He ought to come to know that
greatness that is promised him by his virtues if not by his fortune. Such a man,
however, would surely be a usurper, as Hiero no doubt was.

We are reminded at the end of chapter VI that someone wrote about Hiero. It is
not clear who this someone is, perhaps because Machiavelli wishes to remind us
not of a particular writer but of writers generally. What comes to mind, however,
is that Xenophon wrote about an earlier Hiero of Syracuse,[6] in a work in which
the tyrant speaks against the life of tyranny. Other writers have treated Moses,

Cyrus, Theseus, and Romulus. Moses himself was a writer; he is said to have written the Pentateuch. The true author of the Bible, however, is God.[7] As for Cyrus, he was written about by Xenophon, a point Machiavelli makes explicit in chapter XIV. Xenophon is the only author whom Machiavelli cites by name, if we except God or Moses. Nowhere are we reminded that Moses has written something, whereas Xenophon is twice said to have written about the life of Cyrus.[8] Nowhere is it said in *The Prince*, however, that Xenophon also wrote about one of the Hieros.[9]

Our discussion of the themes of chapter VI necessarily has to be incomplete; we must wait until chapter XIV for further explication, for there we see that Cyrus can be imitated because one can, like Scipio, conform oneself "to the things of Cyrus that Xenophon has written." It is somehow the imitation of Cyrus that is the paradigm for what a prince should do on the highest level. Have not the things of Cyrus replaced the things of Moses?

The question we are left with at the end of chapter VI, then, is, What is the relationship between the writers and the great men of whom they write? The question points to Machiavelli himself, who writes of the actions of great men.

NOTES

1. Richard H. Cox points out that one can read the sentence as an imperative. We are thus, in effect, commanded not to wonder or marvel. "Of Principates, Chapter 6: An Introduction to Machiavelli's Rhetoric of Founding" (unpublished lecture, delivered 6 March 1992 at Claremont College).

2. Moses seems to have approached God as Machiavelli approached "the Prince" in the Epistle Dedicatory. Will Machiavelli come to have the grace to be worthy of "the presence of that"?

3. In chapter XXVI I we will address the question of whether this confrontation is also between political philosophy and Christianity. Does not political philosophy agree with Augustine that the choice should be made against acquisition or expansion?

4. *City of God* IV.32.

5. See *The Prince* XII.75 and, especially, XII.80, n. 23.

6. Hiero I, who was tyrant from 478 to 567. The Hiero of whom Machiavelli speaks in this chapter is Hiero II, who was tyrant from 260 to 216. Xenophon's work is *On Tyranny* (see Leo Strauss, *On Tyranny*, rev. and exp. ed., edited by Victor Gourevitch and Michael S. Roth [New York: Free Press, 1991]).

7. We are again reminded of the great blasphemy in this chapter: is God the author of the work in which Moses is a character (as Cyrus is a character in the work of Xenophon) or is Moses the author?

8. Machiavelli does not give the correct title of the work, *The Cyropaedia*, or *The Education of Cyrus*.

9. In the *Discourses* II.2, Machiavelli directs the reader who wishes to support his opinion against tyranny to Xenophon's treatise *On Tyranny*.

CHAPTER VII

OF NEW PRINCIPATES WHICH BY THE ARMS OF OTHERS
AND FORTUNE ARE ACQUIRED

We have ascended to the highest and most ancient examples and then descended to Hiero of Syracuse and further plummeted to the worst of ancient examples, the princes of Ionian Greece and the Roman emperors after Marcus Aurelius. Only when we have experienced the worst of ancient examples do we return to Italy and modern examples, with which the greatest part of chapter VII is concerned. We return to the theme of the enterprise of Italy, but it is no longer the French who make the attempt; it is the Borgias, Alexander and Cesare.

The example of acquiring by means of the arms and fortune of others is Cesare Borgia. Francesco Sforza acquires his state by "proper means and with his own great virtue." One thus expects the contrasting example to be one who, lacking virtue, would be wholly dependent on others, as were the princes made by Darius and the Roman emperors elected by the soldiers. We discover instead that Cesare's actions are worthy of imitation: the new prince should follow in his path. Cesare's actions are as worthy of imitation as are the greatest examples cited at the beginning of chapter VI. Are they as great, when taken in proportion? Only the Ionian princes and the Roman emperors are examples who seem properly to illustrate the announced topic of the chapter. The true subject of discussion would seem to be, as Machiavelli himself puts it, how one keeps what is suddenly given to one by fortune. Such a mode of acquisition seems to present far more difficulties than does the conquest of a province different from one's own.

We are told that states are like things of nature. They require time to grow and to root, but are they natural? Machiavelli suggests something like an imitation of nature: that in political things one imitates natural things. Once again there appears to be a connection between knowledge of natural things and knowledge of political things.

The shallow-rooted prince who has been placed by fortune must, with all his wit and industry, do the things after he has acquired that other princes had to do before. Cesare Borgia's failure, despite all his prudence and virtue, proves how difficult such a task is. What is given by fortune is itself vulnerable to fortune. Cesare, however, failed in at least one decisive respect: he did not do all that he could.

To be more specific, three times Machiavelli puts Cesare forward as someone to be imitated. First, his actions are said to be the best precepts Machiavelli could give to a new prince. (Clearly, Machiavelli sees himself as a preceptor, a teacher, of new princes or of those who are like the examples in chapter VI.) The second statement concerns the "part" or policy that Cesare undertakes with respect to the Romagna. It is worthy of imitation, and Machiavelli does not wish to omit it since the policy adopted in the Romagna most clearly reveals what a founder must do. Third,

Machiavelli sums up the actions of the duke as those that must be "imitated by all those who by fortune and the arms of others have ascended to imperium"; that is, such actions must be imitated by all those who begin without a good occasion or arms and conquer by force and fraud, bringing new modes to ancient orders. (This describes any private man who has "a great mind and high intentions" and therefore seeks to become prince. By definition, such a man begins by not having the good fortune to be born a prince. Moreover, to infuse ancient orders with new modes seems to echo the suggestion in chapter II that innovations be made to appear continuous with ancient, hereditary orders.)

The actions of the duke thus provide precepts for Machiavelli to give to a new prince, and this praise of Cesare suffices for some scholars to conclude that he is Machiavelli's hero. We are explicitly told at the end of the chapter, however, that Cesare's mistake was to permit the election of Giuliano della Rovere as Pope Julius II. In so doing, Cesare supposed that Julius II would forget past injuries.

The significance of Cesare's error needs to be brought out. His mistake is to suppose that great men act the same way the people act; for the people, as Machiavelli says in chapters VIII and IX, do forget past injuries for the sake of present benefits. The error, in other words, is one a vulgar man would make. Machiavelli twice reports that Cesare is known by the vulgar as *Il Valentino* and that he does seem to have a special relationship with the vulgar. Cesare, in sum, may understand the nature of the people, but he does not seem to understand the nature of princes.

The situation of Cesare Borgia has a certain similarity to that of Lorenzo de' Medici, duke of Urbino. If Cesare's fortune depended on the pope, his father, so did that of Lorenzo depend on the pope, his uncle. Just as Machiavelli does not expect Lorenzo to know the nature of princes, neither does he expect it of Cesare—although it is not clear whether Machiavelli finally excuses the latter for his ignorance. However, whereas Lorenzo and Pope Leo X have to be exhorted to take up the task of unifying Italy, Pope Alexander VI and Cesare themselves drew the sword.

. . .

We are led back to consider the theme of chapter VII. If Alexander and Cesare fail because of errors of judgment, how are we to understand the matter of acquiring by fortune and not by virtue? Cesare did not acquire, because he was given a state by fortune. On the contrary, Machiavelli declares that Alexander VI could find no possibility or occasion to make his son, Cesare, great. It is Alexander who decides on the enterprise, and it is he who is said to have found it necessary to upset the orders that existed in Italy and to put into "disorder the states of all" the powers in Italy, or, as it also said, it is Alexander who draws the sword and so makes his own occasion.

Chapter VII, therefore, is not about acquisition by fortune. Instead, it continues the theme of the natural desire to acquire. The true topic of the chapter is concealed: what we are shown is how to acquire in the most extreme circumstances, where no good occasion exists and where one lacks arms. Alexander and Cesare do not begin their career of acquisition by fortune, and we have been given more than a hint that it is not because of fortune that they fail.[1] Cesare's lack of arms is corrected by deceit: the arms of others become his own. Deceit overcomes fortune, the worst possible fortune. Fortune provided the occasion for the innovators of chapter VI, with the notable exception of Romulus, to demonstrate the virtue of their mind. Chapter VII shows us how human calculation may make its own occasion and thus take the place of fortune. If fortune will not be so gracious, then we must ourselves do what we would like fortune to do. If one born a prince, but without a state, finds himself in peaceful, prosperous, and ordered times, where it would seem that nothing needs to be done, then someone like Alexander or Cesare can upset the existing orders and find greatness in the collapsing ruins.

The subject of chapter VII is the most difficult and perhaps the highest kind of acquisition, when nothing is provided by fortune, where there is no matter ready to be shaped or to receive the form. The strength of his *animo* and his prudence are all that a prince requires; the prince or first man can construct a state whenever and wherever he is. We may set aside the limitations of fortune, for there are seemingly no limits to what can be done.

We have in fact ascended in the discussion of the modes of acquisition from chapter VI. An apparent descent becomes an ascent, for the failure of a Cesare reveals the possibility that he missed. A greater Caesar (and a greater Alexander?) may yet succeed. What such a Caesar would succeed in would be the conquest or unification of Italy. The enterprise of the Borgias is like that of a wholly new prince in a wholly new principate, for they necessarily would have had to institute new orders if they had succeeded in conquering Italy.

We note that the Borgias follow rules contrary to those written down in chapter III for a prince who wishes to acquire a different province. Thus the Borgias destroy the weaker powers, increase the greatness of the church, and invite a powerful foreigner to enter the province. Why do they act on precepts different from those suggested to the king of France, which are, we also recall, the modes of the Romans? Machiavelli alluded to the way in which the king of France acquired provinces that were like his own. The king extinguished "the multitude of lords" within his province, and so does Cesare Borgia. We can only suppose that Machiavelli was making a grim joke when he spoke of how easy it was for France to amalgamate the provinces of Burgundy, Brittany, Gascony, and Normandy. The deeds of Cesare Borgia illustrate what the French kings must have done. The modes of the Borgia are those that pertain to acquiring a province that is like one's own; the acquisition is from within. There is apparently, however, a fundamental difference: the Borgias combine such a policy of assimilation with the dangerous expedient of bringing in a powerful foreigner and making use of his reputation and arms. Is the mode of the Borgias a different and third mode?

The significance of the Borgias's enterprise is suggested most strongly by the digression on the benefits of Cesare's government of the Romagna. He puts an end to the disorders in the province and gains the support of the people when they begin

"to taste the good that was to be theirs." Good government begins with the appointment of "a cruel and expeditious man," who is then spectacularly removed, so that
no blame for the severities falls on the duke. The people are persuaded that only
justice comes from the duke, and they are stupefied by the mystery of the wood and
the bloody knife placed at the side of Remirro de Orco's halved body. Cesare shows
himself always to be a friend of the people, and he amazes them by revealing that
he is capable of such acts. Such are the actions that are worthy of imitation; such
are the actions that the great innovators of chapter VI must have undertaken.

We come back to the point that Cesare fails. The cause is clear: Cesare understands the nature of the people but not of the great, which means that he does not
understand the nature of a prince. That is to say, he does not know himself. His
failure is at first attributed to what one may describe as making inadequate provi-
sions for death. Ultimately, however, Cesare misunderstands the character of the
great, thus creating the one who could harm him. Cesare cannot, therefore, be the
greatest example; that would be the example of the one who understands why Cesare failed. Like Lorenzo and many princes, Cesare understands only the nature of
the people or of low places, and he knows that the people may be both stupefied
and satisfied by a spectacular execution. The greatest example to be imitated is the
one who understands the nature both of princes and of the people. Is that why the
true teaching of the chapter must be concealed? Is it a test of the prudence of
the reader? What will happen to the reader who concludes that Cesare is indeed
the Machiavellian hero whose actions are to provide the precepts by which policies are chosen? Will he not be as successful as Cesare was; that is to say, will he
not ultimately fail?

. . .

We have now exhausted the topics listed in chapter I. That is another reason why
one can argue that we are at a height, though we have discovered many departures
from the orders written down. Are we to blame our leader or conductor for such unexpected turnings? We have ended where we were supposed to end, with acquiring
by virtue alone, which is the highest kind of acquisition. Machiavelli has been faithful, in his own way, to the topics he first listed. The apparent reversals of the topics
discussed in chapters VI and VII are exactly that—only apparent. Machiavelli will
be true to us, but he will, it seems, test our faith.

We may now reflect on the order of the discourse of this first half of the first part
of *The Prince*. The Epistle Dedicatory makes us aware that the conventional surface
of the work conceals an innovative—that is, revolutionary—teaching. Machiavelli
steps forward as the one who understands the nature of political rule simply and understands it as no one else had.

The first chapter tells us that acquisition is to be the topic; thus political rule is to
be understood as expansionist. No distinction between tyranny and legitimate rule is
made. All rule, one concludes, is oppressive, for the liberty or independence of some
other must be destroyed if one's own liberty or independence is to be preserved.

(Machiavelli is silent on ecclesiastical principates, perhaps because his kingdoms are of this world.)

In the second chapter the question is raised, What is a natural prince? The rest of the work may be said to be an answer to this question. We begin to understand the causes of acquisition by examining the attempts to acquire Italy. The invasion of Italy by France is the beginning of understanding what a prince by nature ought properly to do. The enterprise is the conquest, or perhaps the reconquest, of Italy.

The fourth chapter opens up the fundamental question of the taking of the kingdom of Darius, which is presumably still held because it never rebelled against the successor of the conquerors. What is at issue, we have suggested, is the taking of the kingdom that claims rule over all human beings, a kingdom that is also a despotism. We are told, however, that the name of liberty and its ancient orders will never be forgotten and may be called on when an accident or an occasion to rebel occurs.

This discussion leads to the question of new beginnings or new foundings, and we are confronted with the existence of the unarmed prophet and his modes and orders. A new beginning must be made in the enterprise of Italy; we have to see what a new prince must do to acquire a new kingdom there. For such an enterprise one need not wait for either fortune or a miracle. It is the greatest task for the one who knows and understands the actions of great men or how to rule human beings. Hence it is the greatest example one could put forward to be imitated by all those who have a great mind and high intentions and who cannot do otherwise.

NOTE

1. See the further discussion of the role of Alexander VI in chapter XI.

CHAPTER VIII
OF THOSE WHO THROUGH WICKEDNESSES ATTAIN TO THE PRINCIPATE

We come now to two additional modes of becoming a prince that were not listed in the order outlined in chapter I of this book. Private men can become princes not only by fortune or virtue but also by wickedness or the favor of the citizens of their fatherland. Wickedness is to be distinguished from virtue and fortune, as is election. One who conquers with his own arms but against the laws and all morality certainly cannot be called virtuous; nor can he be called dependent on fortune. Here Machiavelli gives us the description of the tyrant, without, however, using that term. In chapter I he indicated in his categories that the one who conquered with his own arms acted according to virtue: why does he now seem to retract that statement? As for election, it is said to be by a "fortunate astuteness," or by a mixture of fortune and virtue. To be elected is to be dependent on others, hence it is by fortune; but one must have virtue to gain the suffrages of either the nobles or the people, the two most important parties in any city. But why, again, did Machiavelli not make these distinctions in the first chapter? Has he changed his mind, or has he failed to mention some important aspect that now makes necessary a reconsideration of these distinctions? The two new modes are mentioned together because both are admixtures of virtue and fortune—a possibility Machiavelli has not raised before. He discusses the first mode in chapter VIII and the second in chapter IX.

In chapter VIII we explicitly confront, for the first time, the question of ascent to the principate through criminal means. Machiavelli carefully states that he will not enter into the merits of such an ascent; he becomes the impersonal observer, stating only that for those who find it necessary such a mode will suffice for the purpose of attaining the principate, and the examples given should then be imitated. His impartiality or refusal to condemn criminal deeds is shocking, for he places a moral burden on his reader: either we turn away from him because he is a teacher of evil or we continue, fascinated by the possibilities he now raises. He has already made us face this choice in the previous chapter, but only in a digression. Here we are confronted with the question of wickedness or criminality itself.

The only possible excuse for such a mode is its necessity—but if it is necessary it is neither wicked nor good. How does such a mode become necessary? Machiavelli is ambiguous. On the one hand, the necessity seems to arise from the desire or the will of the would-be prince; on the other hand, it appears to be a question of natural necessity. Thus he speaks, at the end of chapter VIII, of the necessity that will come with adverse times. In contrast, Agathocles had the consent of his fellow citizens to rule, but he wished to rule without obligation to others. Agathocles, in other words, had risen to the civil principate but sought to transform it into an absolute monarchy. Oliverotto regarded being under others as servility and so destroyed the liberty of his fatherland. Both men could have ruled without resorting to criminal means. How, then, could one say that necessity forced them into nefarious ways? Is Machiavelli saying that it is necessary for a great-minded man with high intentions to disdain to be dependent in any way whatsoever? Yet is not such a statement in itself rather dubious? The desire to be first and under no obligation to others excuses any crime—such, indeed, is what has come to be known as Machiavellianism.

. . .

Machiavelli says that he will demonstrate this mode of wickedness with two examples, one ancient and one contemporary: Agathocles of Syracuse and Oliverotto da Fermo. One wonders why these two stories are put forward. We are apparently meant to compare them with each other, and we note immediately that the ancient example is of success, whereas the modern one is of failure.

In the discussion of Agathocles's rise, it is said that he combined virtue of mind and body with wickedness at every stage. If a civil principate is gained by a combination of virtue and fortune, a nefarious one is won by a combination of virtue and wickedness, not, as we first may have thought, by wickedness and fortune. Agathocles has enough virtue to overcome his low birth and abject fortune, but his virtue does not include faith, piety, or religion, among other things; on the contrary, he commits many deeds against these.

We need to understand Machiavelli's ambiguous use of the word *virtue*, nowhere more clearly illustrated than in that most striking description of Vitellozzo Vitelli as Oliverotto's maestro of virtues and wickednesses. We see, for the first time in *The Prince*, that virtue is, first of all, virtue of mind and body. Such virtue makes one able to see how to take advantage of opportunities and to stand firmly in adversities, certain of one's ability to enter into and to escape from dangers. Such virtue has nothing to do with morality, and Machiavelli acknowledges this point by saying that one cannot call it virtue, because it includes killing one's fellow citizens, betraying one's friends, and being without faith, pity, and religion. Machiavelli's characteristic sauciness or impudence now reveals itself. After having said one cannot so use the word *virtue*, he promptly speaks of "the virtue of Agathocles" and asks why the latter should be judged inferior to any of the most excellent captains. Then he admits that "his brutal cruelty and inhumanity, and his infinite wickedness do not allow that he be among the most excellent celebrated men."

The title of "captain" was first used in chapter VI in reference to Hiero of Syracuse, and it would seem that Hiero and Agathocles are of the same kind. Machiavelli makes us think about the difference between the excellence of captains and the excellence of men and about whether the celebrated men of chapter VI were also captains. We are tempted into entertaining the wicked thought that Agathocles might be taken, as Hiero was, to be (in proper proportion) of the same kind as the most excellent celebrated men of chapter VI. What, in fact, distinguishes Hiero from Agathocles of Syracuse? We are told not to have such thoughts, but it is difficult not to—an all-too-familiar device of tempters.

Two very different understandings of virtue are present here, and the difference between them seems to be that one leads only to imperium or power but not to glory, whereas the other permits one to be placed among the most excellent celebrated men. Without virtue, in the commonly accepted understanding of moral virtue, one may be placed among the most excellent captains. Glory is connected with moral virtue in the usual or common understanding of that term. One must then pay attention to the usual, as the first sentence of the Epistle Dedicatory indicates, if one wants to be celebrated as well as excellent. Does not glory depend on others, and cannot one obtain glory by fortune, not necessarily by virtue? One need only think of the modern phenomenon of what is called "celebrity." To be celebrated requires that one pay attention to what others think of one, and evidently what others think of one depends on one's being thought to have, among other things, faith, pity, and religion. Is the point that one cannot have the reputation for brutal cruelty, inhumanity, and wickedness in general? The massacre of the senators and the richest people of Syracuse takes place in public. Agathocles has made no attempt to conceal his deeds. The difference between moral virtue and virtue of mind and body is, therefore, the question of reputation or the opinion of others, and that very much depends on what is usual or customary. Virtue of mind and body can make one an excellent captain, but moral virtue is required if one is to have glory and not merely imperium.

. . .

Machiavelli now turns to the adventures of Oliverotto da Fermo. He is of "our times," that is, when Alexander VI reigned. Are our times, in other words, especially characterized by the rule of Alexander? We see a little later that a discussion of the enterprises of Pope Alexander and his son Cesare has a special place in Oliverotto's career.

We read of no mentors or teachers in the rise of Agathocles, but they were important to Oliverotto's rise. Furthermore, Oliverotto is never said to have possessed virtue of mind and body, although he was taught virtue and wickedness; he is instead described as being *ingegnoso* (clever) and *gagliardo* (vigorous or bold and gallant) in his person and his *animo*. He is, as it used to be said, a man of mettle and spirit. Machiavelli never says that he is virtuous in any way. His desire not to be servile apparently can be called bold and gallant, but he cannot be said to have high intentions and a great mind. When he decides to take power he is not, as Agathocles was, already prince of the city.

Oliverotto uses those who prefer the servitude of their fatherland. He deceives his fellow citizens, especially his maternal uncle, who was like a father to him, into believing that he wishes to return to the city to claim his patrimony. The fatherless one pretends to wish to reclaim both his paternal inheritance and his fatherland. He therefore makes his uncle and his fellow citizens pay him every office or every due respect, for he wishes both to pay honor and to be honored. The subsequent betrayal is a far greater crime than any Agathocles commits, for the betrayal is not of friends but of his father and his fatherland.

Oliverotto carries out his wicked plans in secret. Unlike Agathocles's public massacre of the Syracusan oligarchy, Oliverotto gives a solemn banquet to which he invites Giovanni Fogliani and all the first citizens of Fermo. He then uses the greatness of the enterprises of Pope Alexander VI and Cesare to persuade the guests to move to a more secret room, where he kills all of them. One wonders what it was about the exploits of Alexander and Cesare that had to be discussed more privately. We have to keep in mind that we too have been invited to speak of Alexander and Cesare, but have we been invited into a more secret room? Has not Machiavelli spoken rather openly of such things? Are we also to reflect on the way a solemn banquet and a discussion of serious things become an occasion for acquiring power? Is there not a violation here of the fundamentals of human association? What fatherland is being betrayed in Machiavelli's invitation to discuss the actions of great men?

Oliverotto strengthens himself with new civil and military orders, and it is said that to overthrow him would have been as difficult as to overthrow Agathocles. He seems, at this point, to have been as successful as Agathocles. Had he continued to be successful, would he have been said to be not inferior to any of the most excellent captains? Moreover, do the far worse actions of Oliverotto merit less blame because of the secrecy with which they were committed?

Oliverotto is deceived by Cesare Borgia, however; he is taken at Sinigaglia, with his teacher Vitelli, and strangled. At Sinigaglia, we see in chapter VII, the Orsini and their allies were deceived first by Cesare's honoring Signor Paulo as Oliverotto honored his uncle and then by Cesare's gifts of money, clothes, and horses—the very gifts listed in the Epistle Dedicatory as delighting many princes. In other words, Oliverotto is deceived the way a vulgar or imprudent man can be deceived and, indeed, as Lorenzo the Magnificent can therefore be deceived.

One notices that Oliverotto merely commits homicide before he is strangled. Once strangled, his criminal deed may be called by its proper name—parricide. That is one of the prices one pays for failure: one's actions can then be spoken of truthfully.

Why is so much made of Vitelli's being strangled along with his pupil? Is there a warning here to those who would teach both virtue and wickedness? But is that not precisely Machiavelli's reputation? Is this the danger in Machiavelli's teaching? Does a teaching in wickedness and virtue incite men like Oliverotto who are clever and bold but not virtuous? Neither Agathocles nor Oliverotto is called prudent. In chapter VI, virtue and prudence were distinguished in terms of the bow and the archer, the instrument and the user. Is there an even greater danger in that imprudent princes, vulgar men such as Oliverotto, will interpret the Machiavellian teaching vulgarly and bring their teacher down with them? And how does Machiavelli plan to avoid the fate of a Vitelli?

. . .

We now discover that one who takes up the wicked mode of Agathocles and his kind (Machiavelli does not name Agathocles and Oliverotto) is not condemned by the laws of God and man to everlasting infamy. He can be saved, if he follows the Machiavellian credo of cruelty well used. Cruelty well used is the means of salvation for the wicked, because it is what leads to "the greatest possible utility." The necessity invoked to justify cruelty is ambiguous, for it is said to be necessary for a prince to secure himself. Is Machiavelli indicating that all princes have to secure themselves in the same way, whether they are an Agathocles or a Cyrus?

We are reminded of the digression on the Romagna in chapter VII, where cruelty was well used in order that the people might enjoy the good. Cruelty is the only means, it would seem, of bringing to human beings the good government they wish to savor or to taste. We are finally told, in chapter VIII, that the end the prince ought to have in mind is to be unchanging in his policies. He is to remain the same in good times and in bad. What is unchanging, therefore, is not nature but the prince's mind or *animo*. The times will change, accidents will come, but the prince alone remains the same, in that he seems to dispense injuries and benefits in the same way, whatever the circumstances. Must one be cruel in order to remain the same in a world full of accidents? Is such security what men wish for from government, and not morality or justice? Machiavelli has said little about justice throughout. Finally, is to be safe in the fatherland dependent on men like Agathocles? It is odd that chapter VIII, the chapter on attaining the principate by criminal means, should contain the most references (three) to the fatherland.

We have in this chapter the clearest presentation so far of what is required if a private man is to become a prince. The founders discussed in chapter VI are certainly also captains, as is indicated by the reference to Hiero's election as captain. If they are captains, they must necessarily do what Agathocles did. Machiavelli makes it evident that whatever moral judgment might be made about Agathocles, he is of equal rank with the most excellent of captains.

The final realization is that salvation for human beings is made possible by such captains. It is they who have the remedy whereby the fatherland may be made safe against both external enemies and internal conspiracies and whereby human beings can correct their standing with both God and man. Machiavellian salvation is political salvation; and at the very end the would-be prince is addressed directly, warned of what he must do to deal with the necessities that will come.

. . .

We now see more clearly why Machiavelli offers the two examples. Agathocles is clearly the exemplar of the mode of founding by criminal means. But what does the Oliverotto story do? First, it certainly shows the extent to which one who wishes to rule without obligation to others must go: he must be prepared to betray his fatherland and his father under the guise of reclaiming them. One must think, I believe, about what this point suggests regarding Machiavelli's own enterprise. Indeed, the whole chapter should be regarded as a reflection on the character of the enterprise Machiavelli has now sketched briefly but completely after seven chapters.

The Oliverotto story also reveals both the danger and the moderation of the Machiavellian teaching. The danger lies in the possibility that those without virtue come to believe that they can attain to the status of self-sufficiency, or the state of he who is truly first or prince. The danger may also lie in the vulgar interpretation of Machiavellianism as an encouragement to such men as Richard III to wade through blood to gain the crown.[1]

The moderation is to be found in the warning implicit in the Machiavellian creed that cruelty must be well used if one is to save one's state with both man and God. To use cruelty well obviously implies prudence; one who understood the Machiavellian teaching as simply a willingness and an ability to do terrible and inhuman things will destroy himself as Oliverotto did. In chapter V the surface teaching of extreme cruelty distracted one from the more moderate course, which is suggested quietly. The danger here is to the one who would attempt, as it were, to out-Machiavel Machiavelli. This aspect of Machiavelli's presentation is peculiar: the harsh teaching is explicit and on the surface; the moderate teaching is concealed.

That leads us to wonder about the contrast between the openness of Agathocles and the secrecy of Agathocles's actions. Machiavelli is as public as is Agathocles; he speaks openly, not in a secret place, about the enterprises of Alexander and his son Cesare. Like Oliverotto, Cesare concealed his actions, as he concealed himself in the Romagna completely and successfully behind Remirro de Orco. I suggest, however, that the most successful concealment of all is that of Alexander VI, for it is he who drew the sword and began the enterprise of establishing a state for his son. Machiavelli lacks concealment, and we can only wonder at his willingness to risk the opprobrium of mankind. Why should he wish to cultivate a certain vulgar view of his teaching and therefore of him? We are made aware of the price he understands that he must pay: he cannot be placed among the most excellent celebrated men,[2] but perhaps he has the consolation that he cannot be judged inferior to the most excellent captains.[3]

NOTES

1. See William Shakespeare, *Henry V* III.ii.165–93, where Richard will "set the murderous Machiavel to school."

2. Consider the ambiguity of the epitaph on the memorial to Machiavelli in the Basilica of Santa Croce, Florence, Italy: *Tanto nomini nullum par elogium* (For such a name, no eulogy). Santa Croce is the Italian equivalent of Westminster Abbey. See George Anastaplo, "Politics, Glory, and Religion," in his *The American Moralist: On Law, Ethics, and Government* (Athens: Ohio University Press, 1992), 516–26.

3. For the significance of being a captain, see *The Prince* VIII.55, n. 4.

CHAPTER IX
OF THE CIVIL PRINCIPATE

The civil principate is attained by a private citizen when he is elected by his fellow citizens. The citizens, however, are divided into two parties, for in every city there will always be found two diverse humors—that of the people and that of the great. A humor is a natural temperament, a fundamental disposition of the soul; thus there appears to be a natural basis for the existence of factions in a city. The importance of these humors is that they give rise to different appetites: the great desire to command and to oppress, whereas the people desire not to be commanded or oppressed. The natural basis for factions, therefore, are the two natural appetites, and from these appetites one of three political effects follows: a principate, liberty, or license.

Each of these appetites seems to tend toward a principate. Each of the parties turns to the rule of one who either gives vent to their appetite or defends them with his authority. The great can give vent to their appetite; the people desire only to be protected; hence their appetite is more just. It is more just, one supposes, because self-defense is always more just.

One expects from the first sentence that chapter IX will describe the legitimate rule of a prince, a civil prince, who therefore does not need to resort to any "wickedness or intolerable violence." But what the chapter actually describes is the natural lack of concord within the city, a lack that inevitably results in factional conflict. Aristotle speaks of human beings as naturally inclined to coupling: one for the sake of procreation, and another for the sake of self-preservation. The desire to preserve oneself leads to the coupling between the more foresighted and the less. These, then, are the natural bases of human sociality. According to Machiavelli, what one finds instead in the city are irreconcilable natural appetites that divide the citizens. In other words, there is no possibility of concord, and the natural condition is one of war between the factions. The great are indeed foresighted, but they use their foresight to vent their appetite.

What of the prince to whom these factions turn? What is his appetite? Is it simply to rule? How does it differ from that of the great? The great are the first to turn to a prince, because they are more foresighted and astute and are able to take steps in time to save themselves. The people can only respond to the actions taken by the great. The great establish one of their own as prince, and that prince soon discovers that he is in danger, for he cannot command or manage men who consider themselves his equal. Thus the prince's appetite and that of the great seem as irreconcilable as do the appetites of the great and the people. One to whom the people turn finds himself alone and able to rule. Furthermore, he can be honest, because he can defend the people without having to injure others. How is that possible? Will not such a prince have to injure the great? Machiavelli ominously suggests that one can very well do without the great. The great are few, and one can make or unmake them, but one has to dwell with the people.

As for the people, it is not said to whom they turn: to one of their own or to one of the great? Presumably, they turn to one who is more foresighted than they are. But is this not a kind of restatement of Aristotle's natural coupling between the more foresighted and the less for the sake of self-preservation? The natural appetite to oppress is wholly replaced by the appetite not to be oppressed when, and perhaps only when, the prince adopts the humor of the people. The people can vent their appetite only under the shadow of a prince. Is the true appetite of the prince then concealed, or does he truly adopt the humor of the people? What happens to the appetite of the prince? Have we not been told of the greatness of the *animo* of those who desire to be princes and ennoble their fatherland? But have not these great-minded men become, in chapter VIII, those who desire to rule without obligation? Is this *animo* or animus concealed by the prince's adoption of the appetite of the people? We saw in chapter VI that the people are the matter that sustains him, that only in forming them is his *animo* realized or brought into actuality. The matter sustains him in several senses, one of which is that it justifies him and his enterprise.

What happens to the humor of the great? Is it simply no longer permitted to exist? Because it is a natural appetite, it would seem that it would always exist; one does not, then, have to provide for the appetite of the great, because it will always manifest itself. Education, the possibility of forming the character of the gentleman, the one who is formed according to what is noble, appears simply to be dismissed. No such possibility exists; what exists are the appetites either to oppress or not to be oppressed. What we have in this chapter is the choice by a political thinker, in his own name, of the many (*demos*) and not the few (*aristoi*). The prince, and presumably his preceptor, is to disguise his mind or his *animo,* his ambition, in terms of the appetite of the people.

The prince who comes to power with the favor of the great has to think of them as divided into two groups. One group consists of those whose fortunes depend entirely on him; the other group consists of those who do not attach themselves to him and whose fortune is therefore independent of his. The first group, or those of it who are not rapacious, should be loved and honored. But are not the great, one must ask, rapacious by nature? The second group is to be divided further into those who do not attach themselves to him because they are pusillanimous and those who must be presumed to be ambitious. Because pusillanimity is, by definition, a lack of greatness, such men are not to be feared. Are they not, then, like the people? The second group is dangerous: they are clearly thinking more of themselves than of the prince, and they only await an opportunity to realize their ambition. One wonders, however, whether there is a true distinction between the first group of the great and the subgroup of the ambitious. Has Machiavelli not already suggested that the great who elect the prince consider themselves his equals? Will not the prince have to judge whether they have attached themselves to him "out of art and because of ambition?" Machiavelli concludes, in fact, that the only thing a prince needs to do is to keep the people friendly.

As always with Machiavelli, one must wonder of whom he is in fact speaking. Is there a reference here to his own enterprise and the response that must necessarily arise to his claim of knowing the highest things? We have already noted such allusions to his own enterprise, and therefore we always have to keep such a possibility in mind. What, after all, is the ambition or the appetite of a Machiavelli or of a writer on political things? What is the appetite of a Xenophon? Must not what is said of the ambition of a prince also be said of the political thinker, of one who "dares to discuss and to regulate the government of princes?" Should he not, with his authority, defend the people and satisfy them, keeping them as his friends? What of the ambition of others who write about the government of princes? Will they not think themselves his equal? If he claims to be foremost among them, they certainly will not be prepared to obey him. Are we to think here, in other words, of the tradition of political philosophy, of the divisions that might appear among political philosophers, and ultimately of the claims of Machiavelli and his place in that tradition?

. . .

The prince is to turn away entirely from the great and seek the favor of the people, whether he is elected by the great or by the people. The people can be ruled; they can be made to feel a sense of obligation and therefore of duty toward a prince who protects and benefits them. As we have seen, the great will not forget old injuries because of new benefits. Such is the remnant left in Machiavelli of aristocratic nobility: a spiritedness that can disregard immediate material well-being. How such ties of obligation may be formed is left to the prudence of the prince, because that may be done in "many modes," and "a certain rule cannot be given."

. . .

The three examples mentioned at the end of the chapter may all be characterized as "great ones" or magnates who sought to establish popular regimes. Nabis restored the reform of Cleomenes, which meant the destruction of the ephorate and therefore of the Spartan oligarchy; the Gracchi also attempted to establish a popular republic; and Giorgio Scali was one of the heads of a popular revolt by the *popolo minuto,* or the lowest classes of the people. According to Machiavelli, only Nabis can be considered a public man; the others were private citizens and were abandoned by the people when the crisis came. Only the prince with public authority—not a potential prince but an actual one—can keep the people loyal. The people require a public or political order if they are to be faithful. We have already read, in chapter VI, that the "nature of the people is variable" and that it is difficult to keep them firmly persuaded of a thing. The prince therefore must have means to keep them faithful or to make them believe. What appears to be difficult to do in chapter VI, however—that is, to keep the people's loyalty—is something that a "man of heart" can successfully do. Machiavelli is far more reassuring in chapter IX than he was in chapter VI. Nor do we hear of arms. Must not the prince with heart be, then, an armed prophet?

The characteristic of the people, we are told in this chapter, is not their changeability but their dependability. Does this mean that, once a people are formed by the *animo* of the prince, the tendency will be to keep or to preserve that form? The true revolutionaries, it would seem, are not the people but the great. The people may be variable as matter is variable, but once formed they tend to remain in that form. Lacking foresight and ambition, they cannot themselves spontaneously seek change. They will change only as a result of some great ambition or *animo.* That would suggest that the prince must indeed see to it that the great are wholly suppressed. The people are to be trusted, yet not trusted. As the last passage of the chapter declares, one cannot, in the end, rely on the people. They promise everything in quiet times; but in difficult times, when danger approaches, there is "a dearth of those whom he can trust." The people remain essentially fickle, and a wise prince has to act in such a way that his citizens will always "have need of the state and of him." Then and only then will they be faithful.

But how is that to be accomplished? We are reminded of what was said in chapter

II: that the natural prince must always make changes in such a way that they do not appear to be innovations. We are now told that the prince cannot depend on what he sees in quiet times—must not the distinction then disappear between quiet and adverse times? As the distinction between the old and the new is to be blurred, so must peace and war, rest and motion, also be blurred.

In what way are the citizens to be persuaded of the need of the state and of the prince, and what is that need? The need, we recall, is not to be oppressed; nor is the need for a protector. Presumably, then, that need will always have to be made very present to the people. Is the difference between Aristotle and Machiavelli to be seen in whether this need is a natural inclination? Is there a natural inclination in the people toward the foresighted one? The answer, indicated in many ways, is that there is no such natural inclination; hence Machiavelli's judgment that the nature of the people is variable. Machiavelli discusses only the transition to the absolute rule of the prince in this chapter, so it would seem that liberty is to be lost. But should one not recall how difficult it is to make men forget that liberty and in how much danger the prince is placed when he proposes to rule a city used to living in liberty? Are these the dangerous shoals to which the last passage of chapter IX alludes? Such dangers can be overcome by the prince if he takes up the people's cause and protects them. Does this signify that the people are to lose their liberty for the sake of such protection? How can one resolve the seeming contradiction of a popular yet absolute prince, who is able to "defend the fatherland and the state" against both the "whole of Greece and one of the most victorious Roman armies"? Such a prince must take "absolute authority in time," for otherwise the magistrates and the citizens will disobey and oppose him. Such disobedience and opposition will endanger the fatherland.

What, then, is a civil principate? We discover in this chapter that a prince, however he comes to power, must turn to the people. It is not simply a question of how one might become prince of the fatherland by the favor of his fellow citizens. A civil principate is one that is founded on the people and only the people.

CHAPTER X

IN WHAT MODE THE STRENGTHS OF
ALL PRINCIPATES OUGHT TO BE WEIGHED

This chapter is the last one on principates. We are to learn how to judge all principates or to weigh their strengths. One criterion turns out to be crucial: princes who can stand up by themselves and are not dependent on others should be able "to put together a proper army and make a day of it with anyone who attacks them." Nabis, tyrant of Sparta, was praised in chapter IX because he was able to withstand the attacks of the Greeks and the Romans. "To make a day of it" is to be able to meet the enemy in battle in the open field. Machiavelli promises to say more in the future about those who can stand by themselves; the rest of the chapter discusses not strong principates but weak ones, those that find it necessary to hide behind the walls of fortresses. One's *terra* (land or town) must be protected by walls, and the *campagna* (countryside) is abandoned to the enemy. The presence of a fortress shows that one is dependent on someone else for one's existence.

Machiavelli, however, suggests a remedy to such weak princes. They are to fortify and to provide for the town and not take into account the countryside; and if they govern their subjects according to what he has said both above and below (one wonders what he has in mind), his enemy will attack only with great caution. The important condition is that such a weak prince must not be hated by the people. How can such a weak prince, dependent as he is, govern his subjects well? In chapter VI, the question was raised as to whether the innovators had to beg or could truly stand on their own; and if they could not stand on their own or use force, they came to nothing. The prince who must use a fortress seems to fit the description of the unarmed prophet, whose greatest weakness was that he had no way of ruling the multitude or the people. Thus, to have a fortress and to rule over the people seem to be incompatible. To have a fortress seems to mean that one cannot rule the people.[1]

Such weak regimes are the cities of Germany, yet Machiavelli appears to praise them for being "free to the highest degree," even if they have no countryside, and whoever attacks them thinks of the difficulties they may have in conquering them. But the main point ought not to be lost: such cities cannot defend themselves outside their walls. Why does Machiavelli praise these cities?

We see that an even weaker regime is to be found. The emperor presumably rules over these cities, but not over those who cannot put an army into the field. Machiavelli does not make much of the emperor, but we should realize that we have arrived at the weakest principate of all, that of the Holy Roman Empire. We only need to consider that the Holy Roman emperor is God's temporal vicegerent on earth to see that Machiavelli is saying that the temporal representative of the Christian order is the weakest sword, the weakest principate: he is the weakest of princes, unable to rule the weakest of cities. Is this principate the one we are asked to judge? The Christian empire is unarmed and cannot force men to obey.

That judgment is muted by the high praise of the German cities. What they are praised for are their moats and walls; their artillery; their stockpile of drink, food, and fuel, enough for one year; their provision of food and work for the plebs; and their military exercises. They appear to be self-sufficient, but they are not. The praise of the German cities distracts us, I suggest, from the significance of what is being said about the emperor, but it shows how a city can maintain itself while under the nominal rule of God's vicegerent, the universal ruler. What Machiavelli promises such a city is that it need fear neither the emperor nor any neighboring power. What power is to be found near the emperor, or perhaps next to the emperor? Is it that power or principate that is the concern of the next chapter?

Machiavelli goes on to conclude that a prince cannot be attacked if he has a strong city, which we assume is a fortified one. The prince in such a city can maintain himself during a long siege, and he will always be able to keep his subjects loyal. The people become obligated to him because he makes them sacrifice for him and because he can keep their minds firm under siege—firm in their belief in him. He is, however, constantly under siege, and he has lost the countryside. Such a prince, we note, has to concern himself with three main challenges: giving hope to his subjects that the evil will not last long; making them fear the enemy's cruelty; and securing himself against those of his subjects who are too bold. Who is the enemy, and what kind of cruelty is to be feared from him? Are we to take the Holy Roman emperor as the example of the enemy, because it is he against whom the German cities guard? We again raise the question, Are we to think of the German cities as an example of the way something like a free city can maintain itself under the claims of the rule of a universal emperor?

At the end of chapter X we are shown how a prince is able to maintain himself in the midst of a prolonged siege. We also see that one of the ways whereby a prince may obligate the people is to have them sacrifice for him. The people are not mere recipients of benefits; they must also give benefits to the prince. That means that they must participate in, or be implicated in, whatever the prince does. And, Machiavelli says, if one considers these things well, he will see that the citizens— no longer subjects but citizens—of such a prince will always defend the city or the free life, as long as the means of life and the means of defense are not lacking. Again, we note the strange possibility of a prince who has citizens under his rule, not merely subjects.

NOTE

1. See chapter XX for further discussion of fortresses.

CHAPTER XI
OF ECCLESIASTICAL PRINCIPATES

One last principate remains for us to consider, we are told, but it is one that has not been mentioned before and for which we are completely unprepared. We have come to the weakest of temporal principates, the Holy Roman emperor, who seems, in effect, not to govern at all.

The concern, as always, is with how one acquires such a principate; we are told that all the difficulties arise along the way but that once a principate is possessed it is maintained without the prince's having to do anything. What does Machiavelli have in mind when he speaks of the ascent to the ecclesiastical principate? Does he not by the very use of the term *ecclesiastical* necessarily make us think of the church? Is he speaking of the election of the pope? Or does he have in mind the way Saul and David were chosen kings of Israel? Perhaps they come to the same thing. The ecclesiastical prince is apparently elected; but does not such an election mean that the principate is attained through both fortune and virtue? We are told that such principates are possessed by either fortune or virtue and not by a combination of the two, as is implied in the ascent to the civil principate.

There is much that is puzzling in the discussion of the ecclesiastical principate. Such principates need do nothing; their subjects never think of abandoning their princes, and if they did think of it they could not do so. The ancient orders of religion are the foundation of these states and are so powerful that they keep princes in state whatever they do or do not do. The state simply cannot be taken away from such princes. How are we to understand such a principate? What kind of subjects can these be, and in what kind of a state do they live? Such principates would seem to be truly not of this earth; they remind one of the spiritual principalities of which St. Paul speaks.[1] Machiavelli tells us that these principates are maintained by a superior cause or causes and that because they are exalted and maintained by God it would be the office of a presumptuous and bold man to discuss them. Nevertheless, Machiavelli says, he will reply if someone demands of him how the church came to greatness in the temporal. Once more one has to marvel at the impudence of the man and at how, even so, he manages to distract the reader so much that it requires our utmost attention to see how he speaks without any respect.

The apparent argument is that if we are to understand the ecclesiastical principate as a spiritual order, then a spiritual order does not govern or defend its subjects—and its subjects do not expect that it should; furthermore, they can never defect from its ruler. God alone, not its human ruler, can exalt and maintain the ecclesiastical principate; and one cannot rebel against or secede from God. How could one, for God is omnipresent and omnipotent? The principal point is that a kingdom that is not of this world cannot, by definition, affect this world; nor can anything in the temporal world affect it. All that one can say about ecclesiastical princes is that they alone are secure and happy because they need do nothing, for nothing can be done.[2]

The church, however, is a temporal institution. Its temporal greatness, therefore, has human causes that can be examined and comprehended. One must conclude that it does not stand by a superior cause or causes. That is another of the impudences of Machiavelli.

Machiavelli thus abandons his announced topic, for, as he says, it is beyond human comprehension. Instead, he responds to "someone" who asks him about the greatness of the church in temporal affairs. What brings that topic to mind? Is the hidden question that of how a spiritual and invisible power becomes an earthly and very visible one? Is it a question that especially pertains to Christianity, which speaks of a kingdom not of this world? Indeed, is the ecclesiastical principate the Christian City of God? What is the relationship between the church and the ecclesiastical principate? If the ecclesiastical principate is the invisible spiritual kingdom, what is the church?

Machiavelli's reply to a supposed interlocutor seems to assume that the church is indeed great in the temporal and that one may especially see how this came to be in what happened in Italy between 1494 and 1513 (despite the fact that the question asked would seem to raise the general and fundamental issue of the place of the church in temporal affairs). The answer is that one must distinguish between the church and the ecclesiastical principate. Nowhere else in *The Prince* (or in the *Discourses*) is the ecclesiastical principate mentioned. We therefore return to the enterprise of Italy, the account of which began in chapter III and of which Machiavelli last spoke in chapter VII. Although these events are well known, he wants to remind his reader of them.

The greatness of the church was one of the obstacles that the king of France encountered in conquering Italy. The church, in other words, is an obstacle to a foreigner who wishes to acquire Italy. In chapter VII, however, the church becomes a means of conquering Italy. Alexander and Cesare, one recalls, do the opposite of what Machiavelli advised the king of France to do. (Note that no ancient examples are mentioned in either chapter X or chapter XI. The last ancient example is Nabis. Have we, for the moment, left behind the modes of the Romans?)

Machiavelli explains the situation before France passed into Italy. Italy was a province, the imperium of which was divided among five powers, one of whom was the pope. These five powers took care that no foreigner entered Italy and that no acquisitions were made by any one of them at the expense of the others. They also kept the papacy weak; but Alexander VI, in his desire to make Cesare great, instead made the church great.

Machiavelli confirms that the passage of the French into Italy was the occasion for Alexander to begin his enterprise. The occasion is supposedly the matter that is given by fortune to one who would be prince, but there is no doubt that Alexander made his own occasion. What is also confirmed is that it was Alexander who drew the sword and used Duke Valentino as his instrument. We also discover an even more concealed cause of the failure of Cesare that was in no way indicated in chapter VII. It is the completion of the story of the adventures of Cesare, and it requires some attention.

We have seen that Cesare is at first said to have failed because of "the extreme and excessive malignity of fortune." The misfortune that befalls him is the early death of his father. Cesare had attempted to secure himself against this possibility. He was not, however, prepared for being seriously ill at the same time and therefore unable to act at the time of his father's death. Worse still, two enemy armies had him completely surrounded in Rome. Had such difficulties not fallen on him, Cesare might have been able to maintain his power.

These difficulties would not have been crucial had Cesare not made the error of allowing the "creation" or election of Julius II. An even greater error was also made. One of the causes of the weakness of the papacy was the short tenure of each of the popes, which prevented them from consolidating their position. The average length of the reign of a pope, it is said in chapter XI, is ten years. Alexander VI did not draw the sword and begin his enterprises until five years before his death: he drew the sword too late. Is this not the principal cause of Cesare's failure? Fortune was truly not the cause of the failure of the Borgias; lack of foresight was. (Is there a concealed teaching here regarding the power of fortune?)

It was Julius, however, who made the church not merely great but also powerful. For the first time in the work, Machiavelli calls the pontificate powerful, and for the first time he also calls the pope, Leo X, "His Holiness."[3] Alexander and Julius both gave the church arms. The church now has now temporal forces, and that is the cause of its greatness. Alexander and Julius are, as it were, armed prophets who have enabled the church to stand on its own. Are we also to conclude that Italy can now be united? That is, the source of the disunity of Italy—factions in the church— has been placed within limits by Julius, who desired to increase the greatness of the church and not that of any private man. The ambitions of the prelates are now held in check by a powerful or armed church.

Have we come to the conclusion of the enterprise of Italy? Machiavelli begins a new topic in chapter XII, saying that he has completed his discussion of all the principates he had intended to discuss. He did not tell us, however, that he intended to discuss the ecclesiastical principate—and he can reply that he has not. The church is not an ecclesiastical principate, for it is now a temporal power that can lose subjects and state.

Thus the concluding chapter on principates brings us beyond the human realm to the invisible power that does not rule and yet has state and subjects. However, that invisible power cannot be the concern of those who wish to consider causes; only its earthly representative, which has now become an armed temporal or earthly power, can. Or are we instead to think that the only true concern is the earthly institution, which acts as any political power does, as we have seen in chapter VII, and that there is no such thing as a kingdom not of this world except in the imagination of men?

. . .

At the end of the chapter Machiavelli expresses the hope that Pope Leo X, un- like his predecessors, will make *this* pontificate not only great with arms but also venerated through his goodness and infinite virtues. Why does Machiavelli speak of "*this* pontificate"? If he means to limit his description to the reign of Leo X, he im- plies that not the church itself but only this particular pontificate is both armed and great. He seems, in other words, to make the relationship between the pontificate and the church as ambiguous as he did the relationship between the church and the ecclesiastical principate. Another possible meaning is that we are to think of that other pontificate, the pontificate of the Romans, and its greatness in arms as well as its venerableness. We are also led to ask why this pontificate is in need of being made great and venerable. The implication is that in becoming most powerful, this pontificate (is this the same as the church?) is no longer venerable. Is goodness necessary for veneration? And is this pontificate no longer either good or venerable?

NOTES

1. Colossians 1:16.

2. For a discussion of this argument, see Thomas Hobbes, *Leviathan,* Everyman ed. (New York: Dutton, 1950), III.xxxix, 407, and III.xlii, 432.

3. The flattery of the Medici pope is, of course, useful for one who wishes to be a client of the family.

PART TWO

OF ARMS

CHAPTER XII

HOW MANY KINDS OF MILITIA THERE ARE AND ABOUT MERCENARY SOLDIERS

Machiavelli declares that he has completed his "reasoning" on all the principates he had proposed to reason on. He has discussed "in particular" all the qualities of these principates; that is, he has given us the characteristics of each kind of principate. He has also considered "the causes of their ill- or well-being," as if he had been writing books IV through VI of Aristotle's *Politics*. And, together with this consideration, he has shown "the modes with which many have sought to acquire and to keep them." Aristotle, of course, is concerned only with how one might best preserve a constitution; he says nothing about acquiring one.

The principates that have been discussed are: the hereditary (old); the mixed (further characterized by whether the provinces acquired are provinces like France or like Asia and by whether what was acquired were free cities); wholly new principates; principates acquired by fortune; principates acquired by criminal means; principates acquired by election; and the ecclesiastical principate. What is missing in this list is the Holy Roman emperor, whose principate is not characterized at all except in terms of the emperor's inability to rule or to acquire the German cities. It makes one wonder whether it falls into the category of the ecclesiastical principate, which is to be distinguished from the principate acquired by election.

The principates Machiavelli discusses are characterized by the mode of acquiring them or the mode of their founding, which also depends on the "matter" of the subject. The Aristotelian examination of constitutions may be characterized as an inquiry into how the noble, the just, and the advantageous may be attained in each. Because Machiavelli is silent about the soul, there is no ordering of constitutions according to the order of the soul. Instead, we have been given the criterion in chapter X of whether the prince can put an army into the field and give open battle.

As for the causes of their well- or ill-being, one must especially recall the discussion of Cesare's policy with respect to the Romagna and that of cruelty well or ill used. Machiavelli does admit that he has considered this topic only "in some part." The principal concern has been, of course, the question of how one acquires, but it has also been the security of the prince or how he may keep and maintain what he has acquired. With the latter concern the question of good government arises.

Chapters IX and X also discuss how the people are to be satisfied and given good government. The wise and prudent prince gains the people and makes them the foundation of his rule. First, a wise prince, we are told at the end of chapter IX, thinks of a mode whereby the citizens always, in every kind of circumstance, have need of the state and of him. In chapter X the prudent prince keeps and holds firm the minds (*animi*) of his citizens, obligating them through their sacrifices for him.

. . .

The topic Machiavelli now proposes to discuss, the third one, is the ability of these regimes to attack or to defend, or to use arms. This is the single standard whereby one weighs or judges all principates and, indeed, all regimes. All states and all constitutions require good laws and good arms. What can be meant, one immediately wonders, by a discussion of good laws, given that regimes founded by criminal means are included in the list of constitutions? It turns out that we are not to reason about laws; instead, Machiavelli will only speak of (in contrast to reason about) arms. He first speaks of the use of arms for the defense of the prince's state against external and internal threats. But, as we also know, it is for the sake of acquisition that Machiavelli speaks of arms. Whether for offense or for defense, however, it would seem to be necessity that makes one reason first about arms. We note that *necessary* and *necessity* are mentioned in the sentence on what constitute good foundations. Necessity rules human affairs, and men need arms to overcome necessity. Laws are set aside by the necessity to have good foundations, and good foundations mean good arms.

If for Aristotle laws are the way in which citizens are formed toward the noble and the just, then for Machiavelli that formation is set aside by the need of arms. Good arms, he declares, presuppose good laws, so one can simply speak of arms, and the question of law is subordinate to the question of arms. The subsequent speech about arms deals preponderantly with Italian examples. What needs to be understood is how Italy became so weak, how it has been "conducted . . . into slavery and contempt." That is the question that must be viewed from on high or from the standpoint of the prince—which reminds us that in chapter XI the church is said to have come to greatness and power in Italy.

. . .

Machiavelli declares in his own name (that is, he follows no one else) that there are four kinds of arms: one's own, mercenary, auxiliary, and mixed. Two kinds, mercenary and mixed, are useless and dangerous. In the rest of the chapter, he speaks only of mercenary arms, for which he lists fourteen characteristics grouped into four categories. First, they are disunited, ambitious, undisciplined, and unfaithful. Second, they are valorous among friends, they are cowardly among enemies, they do not fear God, and they do not keep faith with men. Third, one is ruined if they attack, they despoil one in peace, and they let enemies despoil one in war. Fourth, they have no love or cause to keep them in the field, they are willing in peace, and they flee in war. Central to the list is that mercenary militia do not fear God or keep faith with men. One notices that each grouping ends with some kind of faithlessness, which may be summed up by saying that they leave one naked to one's enemies.

The ruin of Italy is the example of what mercenary arms can cause. Italy was taken by the foreigner with chalk—that is, the foreigner needed no arms but could conquer, as it were, with signs. The foreigner, Charles VIII, was the "scourge of God" of whom Savonarola preached when the latter spoke of "the sins of Italy." But the sins that brought the foreigner, says Machiavelli, are not those that Savonarola believed but rather "those which I have narrated," which are "sins of princes." Princes have therefore paid the penalty for these sins.[1] He who spoke of "our sins," Machiavelli remarks, spoke the truth, but he did not understand what the true sins were, the sins of princes. Who is he who spoke of our sins? Are we to think only of Savonarola and not of another? And who are those who have sinned, for whom princes must pay the penalty?

Machiavelli also wishes to demonstrate the "infelicity" of mercenary arms, and he now uses the familiar *tu:* you, the would-be prince, he warns, cannot trust mercenary captains,[2] for either they will be "virtuous" and "oppress" you and others contrary to your intentions or they will not be virtuous and you will "ordinarily" be ruined. He then carries on a disputation with someone who might object that either of these consequences would happen with any captain who had arms, mercenary or not. The reply is that a prince must be his own captain; he must bear and order his own arms. As for a republic, a citizen must be sent and kept within the laws. The laws in a republic must be stronger than the captain-citizen. This reply is puzzling, for were we not told that laws depend on arms? Must not arms, then, keep the captain in check? Thus the prince has to bear his own arms.

The answer given at the end of the paragraph is that a republic with its own arms is more difficult to bring to obedience than one with foreign arms. In other words, no assurance is given; all Machiavelli can promise is that it will be more difficult, for a prudent captain can obviously overcome many difficulties. A republic, like a prince, must have its own arms; neither must depend on an external power. Keeping one's citizens within the laws begins with keeping to the limits of one's own, especially with respect to arms. The discussion that follows centers on the danger to republics from mercenary captains.

Machiavelli now gives examples of armed and free republics that presumably are to be imitated: the Roman, the Spartan, and the Swiss. The Swiss are especially praised as being both armed and free to the highest degree. Here is a contemporary people who can be ranked with the best of the ancients. Indeed, they seem to be superior to Rome and Sparta, for we have noted how Sparta failed and lost its empire. We discover, with the example of the Carthaginians, that it does not suffice to have one's own citizens as leaders of the militia; the militia must itself not be mercenary. The last ancient republican example, the Thebans, is the only one that mentions Epaminondas, the most philosophical of captains, according to Plutarch. But the Thebans delivered themselves over, after the death of Epaminondas, to Philip of Macedon, father of Alexander the Great, who is one of those whose orders are subsequently praised by Machiavelli. Philip of Macedon took away the liberty of the Thebans, and that raises the question of what happens when the mercenary captain takes power. Will that principate or republic continue to be weak? Are not the mercenary captain's arms then his own? Does Epaminondas fail to provide for Theban liberty, thus permitting the foreigner (in whom is the seed of universal empire) to take away the city's liberty after he becomes captain of the people? The example of Epaminondas leads us to Philip of Macedon, and Philip would seem to be the very exemplar of the dangerous captain previously mentioned. It would also seem that such a captain could, like Cesare, come to possess his own arms and, like the great founders, establish the foundations of good government.

Then Machiavelli turns to contemporary Italian examples, the first of which concern the Sforzas, father and son. Francesco Sforza is perhaps the best example of a mercenary captain who becomes a prince. He is praised by Machiavelli in chapter VII as one who rises from a private station to a principate by proper means and virtue. The son succeeds in taking over Milan; the father forces the queen of Naples to bring in a foreigner, the king of Aragon (Ferdinand), to save the kingdom. What happens is that the kingdom is saved from Sforza and the Angevins, but it is not saved from the foreigner.

The Florentines and Venetians, on the other hand, increased their empire with mercenary arms yet were not endangered by their successful captains. The Florentines were favored by chance because their virtuous captains fell into three categories: some did not win, some were checked by other virtuous captains, and some turned their ambition elsewhere. No example is given of the third category. Paulo Vitelli did not win; he failed to conquer Pisa, a republic the Florentines tried—and failed—to hold by means of fortresses. Does chance, then, not allow a most prudent man to conquer Pisa? Had he done so, the Florentines would have had to obey him, for they had no remedy but to keep him as their captain.

As for the Venetians, as long as they themselves did the fighting and kept to the sea, they remained secure and glorious. In leaving their element, they came to depend on the arms of others and lost their virtue. They had to kill their most virtuous captain, Carmignuola, fearing that which the Florentines escaped by chance. Thus a most prudent man is a victim of chance, and a most virtuous man is a victim of his employers. Italy apparently is not a good place for either: chance is too powerful, and virtue and prudence are insufficient.

As for the Venetians, they suffer a "miraculous loss" at Vailà and in one day lose everything they had acquired in eight hundred years. Chance can express itself in a miracle, which, albeit a miraculous loss for one, is a miraculous gain for another. If there are sins, there are miracles, but not the miracles Savonarola would expect.

Machiavelli now says that since he has come to Italy, he proposes to discuss the question of mercenary arms from on high, which means that he will discuss them as would a prince. He now uses the courteous *voi,* addressing the one who is to understand how the governance of Italy by mercenary arms came to be, a governance that has left her in a sinful condition, that is, ruled by chance and therefore subject to miracles. Apparently, he intends to correct such miracles through an understanding of their origins and progress.

The origin of Italy's condition is caused, first, by the rebellion against the empire, which had the consequence of the pope gaining "much reputation in temporal affairs." These events have occurred in "these recent times"; one wonders how recently these events occurred. When did the Italians turn against the empire, and of which empire is Machiavelli speaking? The struggle between church and emperor divided Italy, and most of Italy then came into the hands of the church and a few republics. Having no knowledge of arms, priests, and the citizens of the new republics alike, the Italians hired foreigners. In other words, the church has been the principal cause of Italy's slavish and contemptible condition.

We have seen that mercenary arms lead to faithlessness. If Italy is governed by mercenary arms, we must conclude that Italy is faithless, without fear of God. No wonder her condition may be described as sinful.

The question of arms raises the question of why Italy is unarmed, or why it suffers for the sins of princes. Italy is entirely dependent on chance, for it has become dependent on arms that are not its own; and this dependence on chance has above all been the consequence of the greatness of the church in the temporal. The question of arms is the question of the religion of Italy—or the lack of it. Whatever it is that the church represents, it is not religion. The only true religion is one that is the result of having good arms; a true religion makes men capable of resisting chance. If one does not have good arms, one is dependent; and if one is dependent and subject to chance, neither fear of God nor faith among men can exist.

We have been shown how to understand the relationship between arms and faith, or arms and religion, in chapter VI, in the discussion of the self-sufficiency of the great innovators and of the dependence of Savonarola. With their arms, Cyrus, Romulus, and Theseus were able to keep the people faithful; Savonarola was not. A people lacking faith is one that becomes random, subject to every accident. And so Italy has been overrun, plundered, violated, and insulted.

Machiavelli speaks of the mercenaries as descended from a school. These are men without state; that is, they have nothing of their own, for they have not shaped any place into a form that is theirs; they dwell nowhere, for they are not at home anywhere. The first thing they have done is to take away the reputation of the infantry. Thus they do not rely on the people; the arms are those of the few or of the aristocrats. They can feed only a few, not the many, and they therefore seek only to free themselves, not others, from toil and fear.

He speaks of these schools as military orders, and one is reminded of the Knights Templar and similar orders. Is one also to think of other kinds of orders that turn away from the people? Mercenary soldiers form themselves, then, into schools and orders; their interests are separate from the people, and therefore they act as do the great described in chapter IX.

At the very end, Machiavelli puns with the word *condotta:* the *condotta* is the contract with a *condottiere,* whose modes of procedure have conducted (*condotta*) Italy into slavery and contempt. We remind ourselves that the meaning of dependence on mercenary arms is that a contract with another, the dependence on the strength of another, is the sin that leads to such a condition of servitude.

NOTES

1. Chapter XXIV is entitled "Why the Princes of Italy Have Lost Their Kingdoms." Is this the penalty referred to in chapter XII?

2. Hiero is the first captain mentioned (chapter VI); Agathocles, the second (chapter VIII).

CHAPTER XIII

OF SOLDIERS: AUXILIARIES, MIXED AND ONE'S OWN

Having presumably learned about the different kinds of militia, we are now to turn to the different kinds of soldiers. To know the different kinds of militia is to know generally the military things, especially the various kinds of warfare. What we have learned, however, is to understand the condition of Italy, or to understand what it means to be governed by mercenary arms.

Machiavelli turns next to the question of soldiers; apparently, what he said in chapter XII about the kinds of militia suffices for his purposes. The sentence that justifies the title of chapter XIII would seem to be the penultimate one: "One's own arms are those which are composed either of subjects or of citizens or your own dependents; all others are either mercenaries or auxiliaries." Soldiers have to be one's own—how is one the possessor of one's own arms or one's own soldiers? That is the topic of this chapter; the concern of the two chapters on arms is the possession of one's own.

. . .

Auxiliary arms, the other useless arms, belong to an outside power whom the would-be prince (referred to as *tu*) calls in "to aid and defend" alongside his people and armies. The first example is that of Pope Julius II. Machiavelli announces that although he could cite many examples, he prefers to remain with the "fresh" example of the pope. The examples in the chapter are indeed predominantly "fresh" or recent examples, but the two central ones turn out to be ancient, one classical and one biblical.

The example of Pope Julius, oddly enough, refutes the point Machiavelli wishes to establish. The pope does not suffer the consequence of relying on auxiliary arms, which is that one becomes the prisoner of the power that is providing the aid. He escapes the consequence by unexpected good fortune.[1] One remembers, however, that the church is essentially dependent on an outside or auxiliary power. That dependence, in turn, results in miracles. Is a miracle the same as unexpected good fortune? Moreover, can one do through prudence that which Julius did through chance; that is, can one succeed by playing off one power against the other?

The Florentines, who, like the Spartans, were unable to hold cities accustomed to living in liberty, called in the French to conquer Pisa. In so doing, they brought the greatest danger on themselves that they had ever faced. Likewise, the emperor of Constantinople endangered himself by bringing in the Turk to conquer a free province. The rule of the infidel and the servitude of the Greeks is caused by the foolishness of the Orthodox emperor. Is the Florentine summons of the French analogous to the summons of the Turk? Instead of Alexander conquering the kingdom of Darius, we have the Turk conquering the Greek republics. The East conquers the West, and the Persian enterprise proves successful.

Thus, Machiavelli concludes, if one does not want to win, he should avail himself of auxiliary arms, which are "more dangerous than mercenary ones." A mercenary captain is a "third person" who is called in. The captain cannot immediately make the "second person" (the mercenary militia) his own, which would enable him to destroy the "first person," or the prince. But if he cannot do it immediately, is it still possible for him to do it at some time? The first task, at any rate, would be to make the "second person" one's own. Once again it would seem that we are to think of Machiavelli's own strategy and tactics.

. . .

Alien arms are to be avoided by a wise prince, Machiavelli concludes. A wise prince should prefer to live with his own arms rather than to acquire with alien arms. Machiavelli then turns to an example he would never doubt: Cesare Borgia. The example of Cesare, however, would seem to contradict the point he is making. Machiavelli's examples in this chapter appear thus far to be singularly malapropos, for we discover that Cesare did use auxiliary and mercenary arms—and to good advantage. However, he always abandoned them at the proper moment, when they became unsafe to use. Cesare began with auxiliaries, turned to mercenaries, and finally reverted to his own arms. Can one build one's own arms by first using alien arms, both auxiliary and mercenary? For the first time in the work, Machiavelli praises the policy of bringing in a foreigner. Alexander VI brought in France, and Cesare is able to make use of his arms for his own purposes. He seems to do by prudence what Pope Julius did by chance. We are, however, reminded of Cesare's dependence on his father and of his use of the church to advance his greatness. Cesare failed, after all, to be truly the possessor of his own arms.

. . .

Machiavelli now departs from recent and Italian examples to turn to Hiero and David. These are the central examples of men who have ordered their own arms. The mercenary militia of Syracuse is, however, like that of the Italian *condottieri*. Mercenaries, ancient and modern, are alike. Hiero depends on no one at all, and we now see that he was to cut the militia into pieces. Thus was the old militia "extinguished," as he put it at the end of chapter VI. Now Hiero is "taken in proper proportion," like one of the greatest examples of men whom a prince ought to imitate. Hiero does not use alien or mercenary arms at all. Cesare does make use of them.

The cruelty practiced by Hiero reminds Machiavelli, somehow, of David. Are we to understand that as Cyrus and Moses do not differ, so too Hiero and David do not? David, the only Old Testament example and the example that is pivotal in the central section of *The Prince,* is like Hiero in at least one respect: he does not use either alien or mercenary arms. Machiavelli is silent about David's being the Chosen One with whom God has made a new covenant. David's fear of God, his piety, is not mentioned. Instead, David uses only his own arms, rejecting Saul's offer of arms. What is suggested is scandalous in the extreme. He who is to be the king of Israel does not depend on alien arms, on a power outside himself. Machiavelli may be indicating one of two things, perhaps both: that the religion of the Jews, unlike that of the Christians, is simply political; or that religion as such has nothing to do with the establishment of political modes and orders, as the ecclesiastical principate does not govern its subjects.

Are we to remember also that there was another Saul, one who can be said to have taken the kingdom away from David? The alien arms offered by a Saul are to be rejected by a David who knows that one must make and use arms according to the modes and orders that are proper to one's own nature.[2]

. . .

Machiavelli returns to a modern example, Charles VII of France. Charles is said to have had fortune and virtue, not prudence. He is clearly a lesser example, but the French, it was said, know the things of war, and Charles knows the necessity of "arming oneself with one's own arms." He establishes an ordinance for both men-at-arms and infantry, but the infantry is subsequently wholly extinguished by his son, Louis XI. Like David, Charles seems unable to provide for his succession. To fail to provide for a proper succession is to fail in one of the most important concerns a prince has to have. The result is that French arms are mixed; that is, they are partly alien and partly their own. Charles is thus more like Cesare than he is like either Hiero or David. The moderns are alike in using alien arms, whereas the ancients, classical and biblical, rely wholly on their own. Mixed arms are inferior to one's own, and Machiavelli declares that the example of France suffices for his purpose; that is, France may be taken as *the* example of modern arms.

. . .

Machiavelli reminds us of chapter III at the end of his discussion of Charles. The moderns once again seem to lack the foresight of the ancients, for it was the Romans who were said to have knowledge of things from afar. He declares that one who does not recognize evils when they first appear in a principate is not truly wise. He then declares that whoever considers the first cause of ruin of the Roman Empire will see that it began only with the hiring of the Goths. Rome is now a principate, not a republic, and the Roman emperor who hired the Goths was not truly wise. Did the Romans—that is, the republic—anticipate the evils that were being born? Or were the Romans not as prudent as we were led to believe? At any rate, the virtue of the Romans is now wholly given over to the Goths. Two references to the conquest of the West are made in this chapter: the emperor of Constantinople permits the Turk to enter, and the Romans hire the Goths as mercenaries.

Machiavelli comes to the conclusion that "without having its own arms, no principate is secure; not having that virtue which with faith defends it in adversity." What is the relationship among these three things: arms, virtue, and faith? If one has good arms, does that not presuppose virtue? And is not virtue that which is required for faith? We remind ourselves that good arms alone apparently suffice, for both virtue and faith are the fruits of good arms.

Machiavelli now quotes an opinion and a saying of wise men: "Nothing is so infirm and unstable as the fame of power that is not founded on one's own." The good prince depends on his own power; things that have only a fame of power, and therefore are without power themselves, have a transient and fleeting fame. What he has done is to misquote a passage from Tacitus. The passage in Tacitus reads: "Nothing of *mortal things* is so unstable and uncertain as the fame of power that does not rest on one's own strength." Where Tacitus speaks of mortal things, Machiavelli speaks of all things, which would necessarily include immortal things. Is it possible for immortal things to depend on a fame or reputation of power? One is reminded of Aristophanes's play *The Birds* (11.1515–1524), in which the gods are starved because no one sacrifices to them any longer. Do the gods have a power of their own, or is their power simply based on what is reported of them? Machiavelli implies that the gods depend on a fame of power; they have nothing of their own, for they are dependent on human belief and worship for any strength they might have.

We must consider another conclusion, however. If the first cause of the weakening of the Roman Empire is that it did not have its own arms but came to be dependent on others, then the first cause of the weakness of human beings is to depend not on themselves but on an external or auxiliary power. The fundamental issue is whether the laws have divine, or extrahuman, support. If not, the belief in such support is one that necessarily weakens or enfeebles political life. Instead of relying on his own arms, the human being turns to illusions, to a power that is nothing but a fame of power and has no power in itself. Such a view of the divine has, of course, become familiar through modern political atheism, as exemplified by Thomas Hobbes and, especially, Karl Marx.

. . .

The end of the chapter leads to what is, in effect, an apostasy. It is also the very center of the work. Machiavelli now gives himself over in all things "to the orders of the four men named above by me." Because the context is that of the ordering of arms, the full meaning of what Machiavelli is doing is not usually grasped. But the order of arms is the order of society or the regime itself; what is at issue is the way of life that human beings should live. It is not God's order that is to be followed but the orders established by the "four above," to which one more name is added: Philip of Macedon, father of Alexander the Great.

"The four above" is an ambiguous phrase. Does it refer to the four who are discussed in this chapter? If it does, Machiavelli would be referring to Cesare Borgia, Hiero of Syracuse, David, and Charles VII. But could he not also be referring to the four founders who were mentioned in chapter VI? We would then have two lists of four, and one name is added to each list, making a total of ten names. Machiavelli may here be playing with Pythagorean numerology, in which four is in fact ten.[3]

The lists suggest that these men are somehow interchangeable. We have been told of the deceptions and cruelty practiced by Cesare and Hiero, and we must reflect on whether all such men act in the same way. Hiero, we have seen, reminds Machiavelli of David. Thus what is said of Cesare and Hiero can also be said of Cyrus and Romulus, and of Moses and David.

This reminder of the nature of the most virtuous captains reminds us also of Agathocles, of whom it was said, "one does not see why he should have to be judged inferior to any of the most excellent captains." We are now considering the most excellent celebrated men, and we have the confirmation that they are as brutally cruel and inhumane as Agathocles the Sicilian.

The final suggestion emerges when we reflect on the argument as it has developed since chapter XII. The question of arms is the question of the religion of Italy, or, more precisely, the lack of religion in Italy. But now we see that the most excellent men depend not at all on any religion; they depend entirely on their own arms and especially, one might say, reject "the arms of Saul," which might be thought of as the most alien of auxiliary arms.

NOTES

1. The success of the enterprises of Pope Julius II is further discussed in chapter XXVI.

2. See Acts 13:14–52, which is Saul's or Paul's interpretation of Israel's history, and, especially, 13:34.

3. One simply adds one to two to three to four, and one has ten. In the article on "Pythagoras and Pythagoreans" in the *Encyclopaedia Britannica,* New Werner ed. (New York: Werner, 1902), 140, the following exchange appears: "Pythagoras asks some one, 'How do you count?' He replies, 'One, two, three, four.' Pythagoras, interrupting, says, 'Do you see? What you take to be four, that is ten and a perfect triangle and our oath.'" One should think of the importance of "ten" in the biblical tradition, and one then sees why Machiavelli gives himself wholly to "four."

CHAPTER XIV
WHAT A PRINCE SHOULD DO ABOUT THE MILITIA

The subject of the chapter is the life given to military service, or the life professed to the art of warfare. To be professed in an art is of course to take a vow to uphold its discipline and mysteries. We are also reminded that a profession is what one makes when one joins a Christian religious community. We have just seen something similar to a vow at the end of chapter XIII. The section on arms, chapters XII through XIV, ends with a description of the life to which the would-be prince must dedicate himself, for one is a prince only if one is professed in the art of warfare.

The prince, in other words, is now explicitly identified as a captain. There is no longer any doubt that all the great founders were captains.

Chapter XIV treats the highest things, for its subject is the preparation or formation of the body and mind of the prince, who is the highest kind of man. The art of warfare is the highest kind of art, for it is what makes or unmakes a prince. A prince should have no object, no thought, no art other than war, with its orders and discipline. Only in this chapter is such a claim made for the art of war.

Princes who think more of "delicacies" than of war, the pleasant things of leisure rather than the painful necessities, are soon deprived of their state and thus become private men. He who would be a prince must always be at war, never at peace, for he should especially prepare for war in times of peace. To be at peace is to lose. The emphasis is placed on losing, not on acquiring. Machiavelli is concerned with the first cause—the first cause of loss of the state—and understanding that cause would presumably lead to understanding the first cause of one's acquiring the state.

The first example given of one who became a prince but whose "sons" subsequently lost the state is Francesco Sforza.[1] Machiavelli uses "sons" in a general sense, so one might speak of the successors of Alexander the Great as his sons. The reference to Sforza reminds us that the Sforzas were the founders of a "school" of arms, that is, one of the orders that conducted Italy into slavery and contempt. Like Philip of Macedon, the father of Alexander, Francesco Sforza was a mercenary captain who took away the liberty of a city. Unlike the successors of Alexander, however, the successors of Sforza and their ilk have lost or will lose the kingdom.[2]

The next sentence reminds us of the distinction made in chapter VI between armed and unarmed prophets. (Indeed, there are many connections between chapters VI and XIV, as we shall see.) He who is unarmed must obey the armed. As good arms imply good laws, so having good arms implies having foresight. Thus he who is armed should rule because he has foresight. Foresight is still the basis of rule, as Aristotle has it; the difference between Machiavelli and Aristotle is that knowledge for Aristotle does not necessarily mean that one turns to arms. For Machiavelli, however, thought without arms becomes subject to armed servants; and that is only to be expected, for unarmed foresight is no foresight at all.

The natural relationship between ruler and ruled is also the relationship between the various parts of the human soul, for the rational part is to rule the nonrational. In Machiavellian terms, if that is to take place, the reason must arm itself. It is impossible, says Machiavelli, for the two to work well together if one is unarmed. The implication is that both parts—ruler and servants—must have arms. One expects, apparently, that servants will have arms, or that the nonrational part will be armed. Somehow the naturally ruling part of the human being has been disarmed—or perhaps it has never been properly armed.

Machiavelli wishes especially to mention one infelicitous consequence of not understanding military things: that the prince cannot be esteemed by the soldiers. The prince must go to war with his soldiers. One may, I think, say that the prince must show that he understands, and is also subject to, the necessities of his soldiers, that his concerns are one with theirs. That is, the understanding of the prince must be directed not to the things of leisure but to those of necessity.

Thus the prince is "never to lift his thought from the exercise of war." He must prepare himself for war at all times, and especially so in times of peace. The first exercise, that of works (*opere*), is an exercise not so much of the body but of particulars. One must accustom one's body to hardships, but the true exercise is in the knowledge and experience of particulars, and that is said to be knowledge and experience of the sites. Particulars are experienced, and there is also a knowledge that permits one to see the nature of things that emerges out of experience. That knowledge and experience are what Machiavelli promised to give to one in the Epistle Dedicatory. Thus the reading of *The Prince* would be like the exercise of the hunt, a knowledge and experience of sites—in this case a knowledge and experience of the sites in Italy, especially Tuscany.

Machiavelli begins with that which is his own: Tuscany, not Rome. Tuscany, of course, is older than Rome, but it can still be found in the hillocks, valleys, rivers, and marshes. The knower of a site must know both the high and the low; Machiavelli now fundamentally contradicts what he said to Lorenzo in the Epistle Dedicatory. It is not true that princes know only the high; they must know the valleys and marshes as well.

The exercise of the body is further described as a "reasoning" with friends, as illustrated by the example of Philopoemen, who speculates on what one does with an enemy on top of a hill. Have we not gone beyond the body itself? It looks as though the exercise of the body involves a certain kind of reasoning, a strategic or calculating reasoning.

The example of Philopoemen is the only one given in *The Prince* of friends reasoning together. Friends who reason together discuss how one meets an enemy on a hill. The enemy is on high; is he therefore a prince? The captain and his friends are to find a remedy for any possible accident that may befall them from such an enemy.[3]

But the Greeks came under Roman rule in Philopoemen's time. Did he not fail, finally, to defend his friends against the enemy? The Romans had the knowledge and experience that enabled them always to have the remedy in time. Philopoemen, Antiochus, and Philip V of Macedon (not the father of Alexander) all failed to save Greece from the Romans. Why, then, are not the Romans given as the example here of those who possess the knowledge and experience of sites? Is Machiavelli's knowledge like that of the Romans, or is it different? To refer to Philopoemen rather than to the Romans seems to place Machiavelli on the side of those who attempted to resist the Romans. We are told in chapter III that the foresight of the Romans led them to make war immediately, not to wait for it to come to them. They therefore carried the war to Greece. "We," the friends of Philopoemen, are to learn how to resist the enemy, and that would seem to be the Romans whom we know (from chapter V) to be destroyers of the liberty of republics.

. . .

The second exercise, that of the mind (*mente*), is the reading of histories and the consideration of the actions of excellent men. If the first exercise led us to the nature of things, the second is concerned with the human realm, the higher one. The first exercise is one of works, of defenses and offenses, and of the body; the second is a consideration of what is humanly excellent, or the highest things men can achieve. Presumably, the exercise of the mind provides the ends for which one exercises the body.

Machiavelli appears to be uninterested in the theoretical consideration of the nonhuman things. He never speaks of himself as a philosopher, and he never mentions such philosophical works as Plato's dialogues or Aristotle's treatises. He speaks instead of works and histories. Thus the Epistle Dedicatory promises a "work," an unornamented one, that will provide the prince with both the kinds of exercise described here in chapter XIV. The work of Machiavelli, *The Prince,* appears to be a history, for it teaches us "how to imitate someone before . . . who was praised and glorified."

The exercise of the mind leads one "above all" to imitate what some excellent man has done. We are, of course, reminded of chapter VI, where "you," the would-be prince, is urged to do as a prudent man is said to do: "Enter into the ways beaten by great men, and imitate those who have been most excellent." The injunction now is to imitate *one,* whose deeds and actions are then always kept in mind.

Next Machiavelli presents a list of great men who imitated a great predecessor and who themselves then became worthy of imitation. It begins with Alexander the Great and ends with Cyrus. We have seen before how these two names are linked with one another. Alexander conquered the kingdom of Darius, that is, the kingdom of Cyrus, or of all mankind. Two other links should be noted: that of the Turk with Darius, and that of Cyrus with Moses.

The absence of Moses from the list given here follows from the contrast made in chapter VI between Moses and Cyrus. All the excellent men deserve imitation, but because Moses cannot be reasoned about, one must instead turn to Cyrus—who is no different, in fact, from Moses. We are therefore especially to imitate Cyrus, or, in other words, do as Scipio is now said to have done. Machiavelli repeats the fact that Xenophon wrote about Cyrus. The life and things of Cyrus replace the life and things of Moses, and they are not different from one another.

To make certain we do not miss the point, Machiavelli declares twice that the life of Cyrus was written by Xenophon and that Scipio conformed himself to what was written. We are not to escape the point that only through histories or writings do we know anything of excellent men. Even more, what we know of Achilles is given to us by a poet, and it is well known that Alexander the Great carried the *Iliad* with him on campaigns. Machiavelli makes no distinction between Homer and Xenophon, except that he does not mention Homer by name. He may not need to mention Homer, but it may also be that the difference between the poet and the historian is that the poet's fictional character is so convincing that one forgets its maker. There is no doubt, however, that behind the names of the most excellent men are other names, the names of poets and historians, of Homer and Xenophon and the like.

Prudent men imitate other excellent men known through these histories and writings. Prudent men are those who know exactly what their virtue is. Knowing their virtue as the archer knows the virtue of his bow, they have as their target the examples of what excellent men have done. An imaginary model, Achilles, can, however, serve as well for imitation as an Alexander or a Cyrus. Writers are able to make us see what excellent men ought to do. The Xenophons, the ones who write, are those who provide the targets at which the Caesars and the Scipios aim. So persuasive is the writer that he seems to disappear behind his work, and only with effort do we realize that Achilles does not exist apart from Homer. Prudent men finally depend on writers who do not seem to have the magnificence or the splendor of the characters whom they make. Those who are praised and glorified are not the true founders, however: the Xenophons are.

Does the art of writing replace the art of war? Or is it the same as the art of war? Indeed, is this why Machiavelli praises art so highly in this chapter, never mentioning its importance again? Prudence is that which subsequently replaces art as the intellectual virtue the prince is especially to exercise.

In chapter VI we learned that the most excellent celebrated men who founded new orders and modes were those who introduced the form, or the virtue of their *animo,* into the matter that fortune or the occasion provided them. The true imitation is the imitation not of God but of these men, which is made possible only by the most excellent writers. The highest life would thus seem to be led not by those named in chapter VI but by the one who possesses knowledge and understanding, gained through hardships and dangers, and who can then reduce these into a book. The exercise of war, which is that of works and the mind, is the exercise also practiced by the writer. Because the princely life depends on that of the writer, the most strenuous, arduous, and daring life is led by the writer. The prince has the models provided for him; but what models does the writer have? If men like Alexander and Caesar follow the paths beaten by others, then the new paths are created not by princes but by those who write of princes, who dare "to discuss and regulate the government of princes," and who know all the places, both dry and wet, high and low.

A distinction was also made in chapter VI between the armed prophets and the unarmed prophets. The one example given of an unarmed prophet was Savonarola. As we have said, Machiavelli thereby raises the question of the founder of Christianity. Was he not an unarmed prophet? But if Cyrus and his like are armed prophets, what of Xenophon and his like? Are they also unarmed prophets? However, these writers speak truly of the sins of princes and what must be done to remedy them, so are they armed prophets after all, the generals who provide the strategy and tactics for the captains to follow in defending the fatherland? Machiavelli, of course, goes one step further: he proposes not merely to defend the fatherland but also to liberate it, to reconquer it. What kind of prophet is he who understands the use of arms?

The term *prophet* indicates one who has spoken with God. Of the captains mentioned in chapters VI and XIII, only Moses is said to have spoken with God. The actions of Cyrus, though not different from those of Moses, were not commanded or taught directly by God. But if Cyrus has not spoken with God, has Xenophon? Moses is himself an author. To speak with God is to understand the governance of the world, especially to understand what is required for the governance of human beings. It is also to see who has been ordained by God to redeem the fatherland.

We know of God principally through writings and therefore writers, and writers are thus prophets—but not the ones of whom Savonarola would speak. Such a reflection leads one to the thought that there is a book, called the Book or the Bible, that claims to be written not by men but by God, who inspired men or commanded them to write His Word. How are we to regard the claim made on behalf of the Bible? One can infer from Machiavelli's presentation that we have a choice. Either the Bible was written by Moses, in which case God is a character in Moses' book, or Moses is a character in God's Book. If God is a character in Moses' book, then it can be said that the biblical writers were so wrapped up in their creation that they came to believe that their perfect being did exist. Even if God is the author, what He writes is not discrepant from what Xenophon has written about Cyrus. God's book has no more status than that of Xenophon's book, insofar as it is concerned with the actions of princes. His Book is to be read as Xenophon's is read. Here is surely one beginning of the modern reading of the Bible as though it were simply any other work.

. . .

That princes proceed by imitation suggests that they are alike or of one nature. Caesar is like Alexander, who is like Achilles; and Scipio is like Cyrus, who is like Theseus, Romulus, and Moses—and like Cesare, Hiero, David, Charles VII, and Philip II of Macedon. The same natures recur. Had Caesar been born in Renaissance Italy, would he have been a greater Cesare? The same natures say and do the same things; the differences between them are accidental, caused by the differences of matter with which they must work.

But if princes are the same in nature, and so are peoples, are the writers also of the same nature? Is Machiavelli like Xenophon and Livy? Is Machiavelli the same kind of man in Florence as Xenophon was in Athens? And are the differences between them a question of circumstance? No conclusive answer can be given, but one is certainly led to think that as one can speak of the most excellent men and their ilk, so too can one speak of writers and their like. Machiavelli does say that the ancient writers covertly presented the same teaching in their works; that is, they all had a similar understanding of things.

. . .

What is suggested at the end of chapter XIV is that *The Prince* is an imitation of Xenophon's *Cyropaedia*, which is called by Machiavelli the "life" of Cyrus. As Scipio imitated Cyrus, so it would seem that Machiavelli has imitated Xenophon. In some way, Scipio is connected to the kingdom over all mankind, or the kingdom of Cyrus. We were asked, we recall, to consider the nature of the kingdom of Darius. The Romans, moreover, succeeded in conquering the kingdom of Darius, or, rather, they established the kingdom over all mankind. Scipio seems to be the exemplar of that Roman success, for he is the imitation of Cyrus and not, as we might have expected, Julius Caesar.

One may suppose that Machiavelli gives such significance to Scipio because he was the first *privatus* (one without office) to be given proconsular imperium by the people of Rome and not by the senate. The young, impetuous Scipio, the darling of the people, would be the very prince on whom a Machiavelli would have to rely. That Scipio was also one of the first of the Roman great men to be touched by Greek philosophy may be yet another consideration. We also need to recall that there is another Scipio Africanus, the interlocutor of the Ciceronic dialogue the *Republic,* who is to lead the philosophers back into the city or to make philosophy once again political philosophy.[4]

Finally, a wise prince can never be at leisure. The language of capitalist enterprise is used. One has to have the capital to resist adversities as fortune changes. Here fortune may still be understood as impersonal chance.

. . .

Machiavelli promises in the Epistle Dedicatory to provide exercise for both the body and the mind. *The Prince* gives us an exercise in the particulars of the events that took place in Italy from 1494 to 1513 and in the universals that lead us back to the writings of Xenophon. Italy, to which Tuscany is central, is the province and the country whose sites Machiavelli first comes to know and therefore knows best; but in coming to know one's own country and understanding how to defend it, one can easily come to know and to understand all other provinces and countries.

Reading a work like *The Prince,* then, is practice in knowing the sites. We especially become knowers of all the proper sites through the continuous readings of ancient things. What corresponds to the exercise of the mind is the imitation of excellent men. In the case of writers, imitation would be the imitation of Homer and Xenophon, of Livy and Tacitus, among others. Writing as they did would thus be the exercise in universals. We are prepared by reading, by knowledge of the sites, or by the work of the body to be able to imitate the most excellent writers or to write as they do. But both exercises are merely a preparation for the true activity: warfare.

. . .

In terms of chapter XIV, the structure of *The Prince* can now be seen as divided into two parts: the hunt, or coming to know and experience Italy; and the war itself. With the first three chapters we begin the exercise of the body, where we start to know the nature of places by, as it were, acquiring Italy. In chapter IV we are introduced to the second exercise, the beginning of the true enterprise, not of Italy but of the Kingdom of Cyrus. We should then understand chapters VII through XI as concerned with the acquisition of the Kingdom of Cyrus and its present occupier, who took it away from the Romans or the princes of Italy. With chapters XII through XIV, the discourse on arms, the armed principate confronts the unarmed one.

. . .

Machiavelli's fundamental difference with the philosophical tradition is that it is insufficient for him that philosophy be simply a conversation among friends. Philosophers must defend themselves, for they find themselves in new circumstances. It is not enough that they come to terms with the conventions of the city and the demands of moral virtue; they must themselves take command of affairs or of the circumstances.

For the first time in the history of political philosophy, the concern is with the strategy and the tactics of the philosophical enterprise, which is, of course, no longer called philosophical. Let us call it the life of the mind. The life of the mind has to reestablish itself by waging spiritual warfare. The philosopher is always a strategist, but now the thinker must employ that strategic knowledge to its fullest extent in practice, not simply in theory. Here is another cause of the emphasis on art in this chapter: one cannot be content with theory; one must practice an art, the art of warfare.

The philosophers are to become a sect; they are to be like the soldiers of Sforza, who did, after all, succeed in attaining the principate—a new militia under a new captain. Philosophy is to be the understanding no longer of the natures of things but of defenses and offenses. Philosophy is no longer to be philosophy; it will be something other, but it will have something of the odor of philosophy.

NOTES

1. Francesco Sforza (b. 25 July 1401; d. Milan, 8 March 1466) was succeeded by his son Galeazzo Maria (b. 24 January 1444; d. 26 December 1476), who was murdered by conspirators. Galeazzo Maria's son, Giovanni Galeazzo (b. 1468; d. 1494), never actually ruled. He was under the guardianship of his mother and her minister, Checco Simonetta, until 1480. The uncle of Giovanni Galeazzo, Lodovico Sforza, the Moor, then assumed the government himself until he was deposed by Louis XII of France in 1500.

2. See chapter XXIV.

3. The only work Machiavelli wrote that is a dialogue among friends is *The Art of War.*

4. We shall have to wait until the discussion of chapter XVIII for a final judgment on Machiavelli's understanding of Scipio, for he there blames Scipio for an excessive pity that led to licentiousness among his troops.

PART THREE

OF THE QUALITIES
OF THE PRINCE

CHAPTER XV

OF THOSE THINGS FOR WHICH MEN, AND ESPECIALLY PRINCES, ARE PRAISED OR BLAMED

The third major section of *The Prince* concerns what the modes and government of a prince should be with his subjects and his friends. One notices the distinction between subjects and friends; it is important to keep in mind that the prince does have friends. Who the subjects are and who the friends are will presumably be revealed.

The emphasis is now placed, as it has not been before, on writing. Machiavelli's writing is a departure from the orders of others; thus other writers have written orders that have had and have imperium over men. He is willing to risk the danger of being regarded as presumptuous because he intends to write a useful thing for one who understands. We are reminded of what he said in the Epistle Dedicatory, when he alluded to writers who produce ornamented or beautiful, but not useful, works. What is being disputed is the question of the highest kind of life, or in what way a prince, he who is first among men, is to act. The disagreement, in other words, is over the nature of man. We are to be given a new understanding of human nature by Machiavelli; or, at least, he will depart from the orders of others in disputing this matter.

The difference between Machiavelli and other writers is that Machiavelli intends to be useful to the one who understands, but not to the one who does not understand. To be useful is to choose the profitable, to turn to the effectual truth of a thing rather than to the ineffectual truth of the imagination. Machiavelli seems to be alluding to the question of the best regime, which exists, according to the classical political philosophers, principally in speech or in image. That conjecture is confirmed by the next sentence, which declares that "many" (many writers?) "have imagined republics and principates that have never been seen or known to be in truth." One knows something to be in truth only if it has been seen. The greatest example of an imaginary republic of which one can think is, of course, Plato's *Republic*. The greatest example of an imaginary kingdom would have to be the City of God, or the kingdom that is not of this earth and is said to be an invisible spiritual kingdom that includes all mankind. The distance between imaginary republics and principates and those that do exist is the distance between how human beings ought to live and how they actually live. Machiavelli seems to acknowledge that there are things that are commonly regarded as good. What he disagrees with is whether one can live by what men profess to be good; instead, one must turn to what is demanded by necessity.

The question of the effectual truth of things raises the issue of human virtue or excellence. What governs the question of virtue is necessity. Necessity forces the human being into an alternation between the good and the bad, or between the extremes. The prince above all must learn not to be good; one wonders whether this means not to choose to be excellent. But why would one choose something other than excellence? That the excellent is an end beyond most human beings was understood by Plato and Aristotle. Machiavelli declares that such an end must be set aside for that which governs all human beings: the desire to acquire. Human excellence is not an effectual truth because human beings act in terms not of the excellent but of the natural desire to acquire. The desire to acquire is what is natural because it is what necessity demands. We are to omit, then, the things about an imagined prince, or an imaginary human completeness that is beautiful, and discuss instead how all human beings are blamed and praised when one speaks of them. That is, what is left unspoken is not, for the moment, to be considered; only what human beings blame or praise when they speak to one another is to be considered.

Machiavelli now gives a list of virtues and vices that appears to have no order to it. The list reminds one of the Aristotelian list of virtues and vices, but it is actually a great departure from that traditional listing. It appears to be a list of ten virtues and vices, as was Aristotle's, and the first notable thing about it is that virtues and vices alternate. A commonly accepted virtue is mentioned first, then a commonly accepted vice. The impression is a lack of a consistent principle in the listing, and no doubt that is the impression Machiavelli wishes to leave. A pattern does, in fact, exist: Two virtues, liberality and giving, are mentioned first. Four vices are then mentioned first, followed by a virtue first, a vice first, another virtue first, and another vice first. The list ends with two virtues mentioned first. Thus the list reads:

liberal (virtue)	stingy (vice)
giver (virtue)	rapacious (vice)
cruel (vice)	merciful (virtue)
faithless (vice),	faithful (virtue)
effeminate (vice)	fierce (virtue)
pusillanimous (vice)	spirited (virtue)
human (virtue),	proud (vice)
lascivious (vice)	chaste (virtue)
open (virtue)	cunning (vice)
hard (vice)	easy (virtue)
grave (virtue)	light (vice)
religious (virtue)	skeptical (vice)

Machiavelli begins the list with two commonly accepted virtues, then follows that with twice as many accepted vices. He then alternates between virtue and vice. One can say that Machiavelli is not simply an amoralist or one who mocks all morality. Rather, he wants to be able to break with the generally accepted views of the good and the bad, or, as he says, to be able to be good and bad depending on what is necessary to do. Always being good will lead one to destruction, but so will always being bad.

Avarice stands alone in the list as having no alternative; it is therefore neither a virtue nor a vice. We have heard of man's natural desire to acquire: there is simply no alternative to it. There is, moreover, an emphasis on Machiavelli's speaking Tuscan, and we are reminded of what he has said of the study of Tuscan sites. It is also a reminder that he is not therefore speaking the classical tongues of the tradition. The reference to Tuscany in connection with the word *avarice* takes us to something older than Rome. The primordial passion seems to be connected to the primordial origins of Italy. Is the novel also a return to the oldest Italian, and human, stratum of all?

When one compares the Machiavellian list with the Aristotelian, one notes the absence of the virtues of magnificence and magnanimity. Magnificence is simply absent: we have, after all, seen the dubiousness of magnificence in the Epistle Dedicatory. And magnanimity seems to have been replaced by humanness. The only recognizable Aristotelian virtue is liberality, the first virtue Machiavelli discusses—to what effect we shall see in chapter XVI.

Particular virtues and vices are discussed until chapter XIX, when Machiavelli switches to generalities. He ends the discussion of specific virtues and vices with faith and faithlessness. It would seem that the list has been sufficiently comprehended in chapters XVI through XVIII.

The concern of the prince must be to keep the state; nothing else is significant. Human conditions do not permit human beings simply to be good: what is done by necessity cannot, of course, be regarded as good or bad. The greater the demands of necessity, the greater the importance of the state and the political and the less that can be given to human excellence. The prince must conform to what seems to be vice itself, and only then will security and the good be obtained for his subjects and his friends. The prince must be willing to be less than excellent, or not excellent at all, for the sake of himself and of others. Writers have been mistaken in their orders in not acknowledging this truth. They have wished princes to have every praiseworthy quality, even if having such loses them the state. Have princes tended also to wish to be good? Otherwise, why must they be counseled that they need especially to learn how to be not good and to use it? This is a reversal of the usual "Mirrors of Princes," which have counseled the prince to have every virtue. But would one who understands require such counsel, for would he not also understand the requirements of necessity? Is there a fastidiousness that must be overcome, an unwillingness to be less than excellent or to give up the delusion that one can be excellent—which is a fastidiousness fostered by the illusions of imaginary republics or principates?

. . .

In rejecting the imagination of a thing for the effectual truth, Machiavelli rejects the power of images to form the soul. We have noted that he never mentions the soul in *The Prince*. He thus silently denies that the soul is a cause of human action. Since the soul is a final cause, he turns only to efficient causes. In Aristotle's description, what is wished for is presented by the intellect to the desiring part of the soul as an image. The image evokes an appetite, and the appetite then moves the organic parts. Desire formed by the image might be called intellectual desire. Aristotle thus speaks of the power of rhetoric and poetry, both of which move men to action. What Machiavelli denies is the efficacy of the image to form the desiring or nonrational part of the soul. Men's desires are moved by the external forces of necessity, not by images. Here is the great dividing line between the ancient political philosophers and Machiavelli. Can the images form the soul? Is the intellect therefore able to move men into action? Or must one work with the causes external to man before which the images are nothing?

The wickedness of advocating that one, especially the prince, be vicious is among those things that have given Machiavellianism its dark reputation. Machiavelli understood the importance of appearances, as he makes evident in chapter XVIII. Why, then, does he permit himself to say that one must learn to be wicked and do vicious things? To act according to necessity is to be neither good nor wicked, but instead of presenting a decent surface for a harsh teaching, he seems to take a certain delight in saying what no one has dared to say.

In Thucydides, and classical writers generally, the harsh teaching is always concealed under a decent surface. Machiavelli's surface is an indecent one. He speaks of indecent things in his own name. Why does Machiavelli bring shocking things to the surface? An example of such a shocking thing is the story of Remirro de Orco. Another is what is said of Moses, and certainly there is the ambiguity regarding Agathocles. At the same time, Machiavelli conceals a far more moderate teaching beneath the shocking surface, as we have seen and will further see.

Why does Thucydides speak decently? For most men, it is far better that they follow the common opinion as to what is good and bad than otherwise. The surface decency, or what is called the preservation of appearances, has the important purpose of not misleading those who are apt to misunderstand what is truly necessary and what is not. Human reason is weak, and human passions can be as irrational and destructive a force as earthquakes, floods, or volcanic eruptions. Thus decency must be preserved to help keep the passions in check. Not everything must be said; not everything must be brought to light. What cause is there for putting the beastly aspect of human life on display? Why reduce men to the necessary part of their lives? Human beings need a certain forgetfulness of their part of human life. Cicero, for example, speaks in terms of nature's contriving to keep covered certain parts and functions, almost as if clothes or coverings were natural to human beings. Decency follows the natural order. We need to keep our minds off our nakedness if we are to become fully human.[1]

What is Machiavelli's purpose in bringing the indecent things to light? One possibility, as suggested in chapter VIII of this book, is that he wishes to test his readers. Some will be horrified by the surface teaching; these will be the disarmed. What of those who will be attracted by the surface teaching? What such blood-thirsty ones will miss and will not see is the concealed moderate teaching. The bloodthirsty will destroy themselves because they will not be prudent. But this is a most dangerous course to follow, for cannot such men do great harm as they are tempted to extreme and violent deeds?

Another possibility is that Machiavelli believes we have forgotten something about human nature that needs to be restored. Something has happened to make us forget necessities, and Machiavelli proposes to remind us of it in the sharpest way he can. He dares to do what has never been done before, and he is willing to risk in-famy to do so. As he says, one should not concern oneself with incurring the in-famy of those vices without which it would be difficult (but not impossible?) to save the state.

Who would be attracted by the indecencies? One's immediate conjecture is that it would be especially the young who would not understand. The young always like to hear of forbidden things, and they delight in the violent and the extreme. And is not the taste for the violent and the extreme a vulgar taste? Does not Machiavelli therefore cater not to the taste for the noble but to the taste of the vulgar?

NOTE

1. See *De officiis* I.xxxv (127).

CHAPTER XVI

OF LIBERALITY AND PARSIMONY

The Machiavellian reversal of the traditional understanding of the virtues and the vices is first and especially exemplified by his treatment of the virtue of liberality. That Machiavelli chooses to begin with liberality is itself revealing, for the underly-ing question is whether human beings are able to be free of acquisitiveness. Aristo-tle describes liberality as the disposition toward the spending or giving of wealth. It is a virtue that depends on our being free of either a too great concern or an uncon-cern with wealth. Liberality is the mean between stinginess and prodigality. Above all, it is the virtue of the free man—hence its name—whose most immediate task it is to run a free household and therefore to manage property.

The first step Machiavelli takes in his reversal is to show that the virtue of liberal-ity is indistinguishable from the vice of prodigality and is thus the same. To be held to be liberal, to gain a reputation for liberality, one must be sumptuous and therefore prodigal. The "effectual truth" of liberality is prodigality, for one cannot be liberal in the Aristotelian sense and be held to be liberal. That is, to be truly liberal is to have no reputation for it, or in fact to be thought stingy. Because a ruler must have an effect, if he wishes to be thought liberal, he must perforce be prodigal. The virtue of liberality thus leads to an even greater vice, for if one is prodigal one will be forced to burden the people extraordinarily and thus commit injustice. An extraordinary burden is one that goes beyond all reasonable expectation; a more than human burden is exacted by those princes who most wish to be thought liberal or, more generally, who wish to be thought virtuous.

. . .

If liberality is a vice, then stinginess turns out to be a virtue. The prudent prince will not escape the infamy of the name of stinginess. Machiavelli states this point carefully: to become known for liberality is harmful; the difficulty with the virtues and vices is that the people's understanding will always be defective. They will always be in error as to what to regard as a virtue or a vice.

Stinginess is thus preferable to liberality, because it is more just. The people are not oppressed when the prince is thought to be stingy. To wish to seem to be virtuous leads to injustice; not to care about seeming to be vicious leads to justice. And has not Machiavelli just shown us that he does not care about seeming to be vicious?

He offers three modern examples of stingy rulers. His Holiness, His Most Christian Majesty, and His Most Catholic Majesty are all reputed to be stingy. Modern rulers have learned to avoid liberality so that they may wage war and undertake enterprises. Does their lack of liberality also permit them to be just to the people?

Caesar is the example of someone who attained the principate by liberality. Unlike modern rulers, Caesar would seem to have been effectively liberal. Machiavelli responds that Caesar was liberal on his way up to the principate, but once he attained it he had to temper his spending. A second objection is raised by an interlocutor who asks whether there have been examples of those who have been liberal toward their armies. Machiavelli responds that one can be effectively liberal with that which belongs to others, especially if one depends on one's armies. One has to be liberal toward one's soldiers. Liberality, then, is necessary for those who are leading armies; it is apparently not possible for one who is at the head of a society that is at peace. He speaks, we note, of a prince with his armies. He says nothing of republics and whether they can be liberal.

Thus taking property through conquest, or practicing injustice toward others, permits one to have the virtue of liberality. A great injustice makes possible the exercise of a virtue. We begin to understand what was said in chapter XV, that conforming to what seems to be virtue will lead to ruin, whereas conforming to what seems to be vice succeeds in the security and the good. One cannot keep one's own—that is, be just—without being vicious (stingy). Neither can one be virtuous (liberal) without being rapacious or unjust. One cannot avoid being vicious. The middle way is not possible; the prince must take one of the extremes.

The cause of this condition is the people and their lack of understanding. Virtue and vice must be understood in terms of how the people perceive them, not in terms of what they are in themselves. Effective truth is the truth as it affects the people. Indeed, chapters XVI through XVIII are especially concerned with the people and how things appear to them. The question of virtue and vice is principally concerned not with the qualities of the prince but with how these qualities are perceived by the people and how the perception affects them.

The prince cannot be virtuous because of the people. So that the people may keep their own he must give up his desire to be virtuous. Prudence, but not an Aristotelian prudence, replaces virtue. Machiavellian prudence is what permits the prince to be good and not good, as necessity requires. Is it difficult for princes to give up their desire to be virtuous? It would seem so, for why else would they need to be persuaded from it?

The last three examples in the chapter are ancient ones. Cyrus, we now discover, was a great giver of that which belonged to others. Scipio was said to have imitated Cyrus in chastity, affability, humanity, and liberality. We now see that what permitted these virtues to exist was the vice of rapacity. The ancients were rapacious; the moderns stingy. The ancients were liberal; the moderns just. Have the moderns— that is, the Christian kings—failed to be as liberal to the people as Cyrus, Caesar, and Alexander? The latter three are the great universal conquerors, the men who proposed to rule all of mankind or to acquire all of mankind, and all are said to be at the heads of armies. We note that Machiavelli is silent about the possibility of a society at peace or at rest.

Machiavelli concludes, virtuously and strangely, that a prince should not try to have the name of liberal and thereby incur the name of rapacious. But the three examples he has given us of liberality and rapacity are among the most excellent celebrated men. The greater names are of those who are reputed to be liberal, not those who are reputed to be stingy. Machiavelli never mentions the virtue of justice; it is implied, rather, in the vice of stinginess. One is not thought of as just if one does not take what belongs to others; instead, one is thought of as stingy.

. . .

In fact, Machiavelli has not distinguished between liberality and giving, stinginess and rapacity. A virtue appears to be the same as a vice, and a vice is the same as a virtue. Liberality is effectively the same as prodigality, stinginess is justice, and injustice or rapacity is liberality.

Are modern or Christian princes then better than the ancients? The ancient examples are of those who are liberal; the moderns cannot be liberal in the way the ancients could. Is there not an ambiguity at the end of this chapter? Cyrus, Caesar, and Alexander were great givers and were therefore reputed to be liberal. Yet we are warned against incurring the name of liberality and urged not to care about the name of stingy, as the modern princes were reputed to be stingy. Yet which examples are better to follow, the liberal ancient conquerors at the heads of armies or the stingy Christian princes, whose armies are not mentioned?. The stingy rulers are stingy in order to wage war. Why are the latter not liberal with the goods of others?

Does the reference to waging war indicate that stinginess and rapacity cannot in fact be distinguished from one another and that ancient and modern princes cannot also be distinguished in this respect?

The true distinction is, of course, whether one spends one's own or that of others. That point is somewhat obfuscated at the end of the chapter, which leaves the impression that what is commended by Machiavelli is stinginess or justice. Does he not, in fact, commend liberality?

CHAPTER XVII

OF CRUELTY AND PITY: AND IF IT IS BETTER TO BE LOVED
THAN FEARED, OR THE CONTRARY

The moral reversals that now take place are that cruelty results in peace and faith and that pity or piety (*pietà*) leads to murders and rapine. The example is Cesare Borgia's establishing good government in the Romagna, satisfying and stupefying the people in a particularly striking way. Such displays are required if one is truly to show *pietà*. Civil disorder is far more destructive than is any "rare example." Spectacular executions are necessary if one is to avoid the truly cruel disorders, for these destroy whole bodies of men.

Pietà in the Italian denotes piety as well as pity. Machiavelli plays on this ambiguity; thus cruelty, not piety, is what reduces the Romagna to peace, faith, and unity. Cruelty is the true foundation of community, not piety.

Machiavelli states his belief in cruelty well used in chapter VIII. Cruelty is what brings about one's salvation, for it reconciles one with both men and God. Thus chapter XVII would seem to be Machiavelli's own faith or religion. We shall learn in chapter XVIII how to keep that faith.

A new prince, especially, cannot avoid the name of cruelty. The question, once again, is that of reputation. Only those who can consider the matter well will see the truth regarding cruelty. A poet is cited as one who understands this point. The poet, of course, speaks not in his own name but through the mouth of a character. But the poet now becomes the mouth through which Machiavelli speaks. Machiavelli speaks through the mouth of Virgil; does he thus replace Virgil? This is the first time that a new prince has been mentioned since chapter VI.

Dido's words are an assurance to the Trojans that she means them no harm. She offers them aid and safety, as well as the possibility of settlement. Her words may be of harsh things, but she acts kindly and soon comes under the domination of love. We are reminded of the difference between poet and character, between word and deed. Dido chooses love; Virgil's hero, Aeneas, does not. And we ought to remember that Virgil is the guide of another poet, who has also spoken through the mouth of Virgil. Is that work to be kept in mind as we consider the question of love and fear?

. . .

The prince must above all show himself to be a serious man: one who is neither too confident nor too diffident and one who proceeds with prudence and humanity. Only from such a ruler will cruelty be accepted as necessary. Above all, the virtue of humanity is possible only if cruelty is well used. Machiavelli places the emphasis on prudence. Prudence alone can keep the prince from excess or defect, but prudence must be accompanied by the quality of humanity.

A dispute arises, Machiavelli says, "from this." To what does he refer, the question of cruelty generally or the prudence of the prince? Or to both, for only a prudent prince will know how and when to be cruel? The dispute is over whether it is better to be feared or loved. Is this not a peculiarly Christian dispute? The classical political philosophers put the question of obedience to the prince in terms not of love or fear but of foresight and of the noble, the useful, and the good. And is not the choice between fear and love in fact a choice between the Old and the New Covenants? Must the question be raised in a new way because of circumstance? It is not the way Machiavelli himself would have spoken; he comes to it only because of the dispute that has arisen. He declares that it would be good to mix the two together if it were possible, but because it is not, we must choose safety—and it is safer to be feared than to be loved.

The cause lies in the nature of human beings. They are especially lovers of gain or of acquisition, and everything they do is in terms of their self-interest, not that of the one whom they say they love. Words of love are easy to say and will always be said when need is at a distance. The prince cannot rely on words. As a prophet must be armed in order to hold a people to a belief, so must men generally be forced to keep their words. An armed faith is the same thing as a cruel faith.

A prince who does not depend on men's words and who does not lack other preparations is one who acquires friends with nobility and greatness of mind. Chapters IX and X showed how a prince unites a people with himself. He must not only benefit them but also make them suffer for him. Friends, however, are to be spent when the time comes; that is why one acquires them. Does not the prince thus act the way all men act? He too breaks words of love on every occasion of his utility. And because he does not fear, would he not be the greatest breaker of faith? In what way is the prince of noble mind—in the greatness of his enterprises, in his capacity to impose his *animo* on a people?

If one cannot be both feared and loved, then one can be feared and not hated. One is not hated if one is prudent and has a great and noble mind. The rule to follow, which will always succeed, is to abstain from the goods and the women of one's citizens and subjects. A general rule that always works seems to replace prudence and nobility.

To proceed against the blood of someone is safe, if one does not take away his patrimony. To proceed against the blood does not only mean to kill someone, it also means that one destroys a lineage, a network of customary affection and obligation. We are then confronted with one of the most shocking of Machiavellian dicta: the death of a father is more easily forgotten than is the taking of property. Human beings pay greater heed to property than to blood. The human need for property is infinite; the need to do something about the blood is very rare and quickly disappears.

Ties of blood, and everything they imply, do not have as powerful a hold on human beings as does the need of property for self-preservation. Machiavelli's strongest statement so far about the fundamental character of self-preservation is made here in chapter XVII. The necessity for self-preservation is the cause of human fickleness, hypocrisy, deceit, and cowardice. But if it is by necessity that they are so, they cannot then be blamed. The prince cannot base himself on blood and love; he must, instead, turn to property or goods. If he is able to maintain the patrimony of human beings, he does not have to concern himself with the blood of someone or the death of a father.

The importance of property is connected to the importance of human need. Human beings cannot preserve themselves without acquiring property. That need is infinite, and the prince must defend himself against the boundlessness of that need.

Rule over armies, composed of many men of many nations, demands that the prince be inhumanly cruel. Of Hannibal's wonderful actions, the most wonderful is that there was never any dissension in his army. Hannibal shows that one can be inhumanly cruel and yet have infinite virtues. We now see that one can be venerated and terrible, rather than venerated and good, as, in chapter XI, he called on Pope Leo X to be. Indeed, without cruelty the virtues of Hannibal would have had no effect; cruelty is what makes virtue or truth and goodness effectual. Liberality, we see, depends on an apparently inhuman cruelty.

Machiavelli now mentions how mistaken the writers have been about the principal cause of Hannibal's action. It is the only place in *The Prince* where he openly criticizes writers. Writers (including Virgil?) have not understood why cruelty is needed to bring about the effect they admire. In chapter XVIII the writers reveal themselves to be of the vulgar.

The question here is once again that of rule over armies. Liberality and cruelty are the two qualities most necessary to a prince at the head of an army, especially an army composed of men of many nations warring in alien lands. One would now have to remember what was suggested in chapter XIV about what the highest human life might be. We are here speaking of the three highest types of human beings, of whom Hannibal and Scipio are the two clearest alternatives.

Scipio is said to be one of the rarest of men in the memory of all mankind. Is Machiavelli praising him, or are we to wonder whether a rare man is an extraordinary one, with extraordinary modes? We see that his excessive *pietà* corrupted the military orders of Rome, which is the corruption of the republic itself; and he does not avenge or correct human wrongs but lets them go on. Is it not cruelty well used that is required to correct human wrongs? This is the man, we remember, who imitated Cyrus. Was Cyrus also characterized by excessive pity? Or should we think of other orders that show excessive pity or compassion for human beings but do not correct human injustice?

Scipio would have failed in his rule, but because he had a senate to correct him, his excessive pity was hidden and he was brought to glory. The senate provided the government that Scipio could not. Can excessive pity be corrected by a properly ordered constitution? As long as a senate exists, will it always be possible to hide the fault of a Scipio and bring him to glory? But perhaps it is not, after all, an institution that saves Scipio but a man, Fabius Maximus, who is said to have corrected Scipio in the senate. Was Fabius concealed in the senate? What are we to conclude? Are we to see that behind the brilliant success and glory of a Scipio are the prudent and humane men who know how to punish and to take vengeance? Or perhaps there is only one man. But was it not Scipio who brought the Second Punic War to an end, defeating Hannibal at Zama? We are left with no indication of how to answer this last question.

. . .

If Hannibal's nature is difficult and Scipio's is easy, is Fabius a mean of the two? Of the three (are we to think of them as the three principal kinds of men who head armies?), only Hannibal can be said to be self-sufficient. One does not know whether Fabius can rule by himself or must work through a political institution, where what he does is screened from immediate view. Or, again, are we to see that it is the senate, not Fabius, that saved Scipio?

Machiavelli concludes that the prince must depend on his own, and he must therefore choose to be feared, not loved. Fear belongs to the human condition; love does not, for love assumes that another will take as much interest in one as one would oneself. To love a neighbor as one loves oneself is a demand that human beings cannot meet; that would be to place one's faith entirely in the other or to ask too much of the human condition. Has not the choice thus apparently been made for Hannibal's cruelty? But, once again, are we not to think of the more moderate mode of the senate?

<hr/>

CHAPTER XVIII

IN WHAT MODE PRINCES OUGHT TO KEEP FAITH

To maintain faith is to live with integrity, that is, not to hide something of oneself from others but to be open in one's words and deeds. Everyone understands that to keep faith is praiseworthy—again, there is a common recognition of moral virtue. Why is there such a common understanding, one wonders? We shall have to see whether Machiavelli has an answer for this question.

Nonetheless—Machiavelli's *nondimanco* always introduces some reversal that may go against all opinion and all reason—one sees that princes have done great things by not keeping faith and with cunning have befuddled men's brains. Cunning has proved to be more successful than loyalty.

The reader is now addressed, for we now have to consider a theoretical point. There are two kinds of fighting, one that is proper to man and one that is proper to beasts, and one is forced to resort to the second. As one hunts beasts, so at times one must hunt man. The metaphor of the chase in chapter XIV may not be a metaphor after all. A prince must know the nature of both beast and man and must use one or the other, according to the need. One without the other is not durable. One cannot simply be beastly or human; one has to alternate between the two, using each to strengthen the other.

. . .

Writers have become more prominent since chapter XIV, and ancient writers are now said to have taught covertly what Machiavelli here teaches openly and with his own mouth, not that of Dido or Virgil or of Achilles or Homer. What has been covertly taught is that man must learn from one who is half beast, not from one who is either half or wholly divine. Chiron is called a preceptor (*precettore*), a term used only once before, in chapter VI, where God is said to be the preceptor of Moses. We are no longer to see the human being in biblical terms.

Chiron is a centaur, half horse and half man. Xenophon, in the *Cyropaedia* (IV.iii), describes how Cyrus urges the Persians to turn to cavalry, and Chrysantas responds by speaking of his envy of the centaur and how a horseman is in fact a centaur, combining human foresight with the physical senses, speed, and strength of the horse. To be a horseman, however, is better than to be a centaur, for one can remain human and dismount from the horse. The horseman can take apart the two natures; the centaur cannot. And to be a horseman, says Chrysantas, is to have wings.

Thus what gives wings to man is not the soul but his animal body. Only by learning to use the body will man rise and be like the gods. But to be a god one must look down, not up, and in knowing how to use his heaviness he will become light and swift. The wings of man are not his soul but the animal body—if its nature is known and used properly. That knowledge of the body begins with the ancient writers. Modern writers, we surmise, know nothing of it, perhaps because of their preceptor.

But the prince is not a centaur; instead, his beastliness is a mixture of the fox and the lion. Man is doubly a monster. Machiavelli speaks mostly of the fox, not of the lion, and to be a fox especially means not to observe faith. A fox always knows how to cover his tracks, however, for to be a fox is to be a great hypocrite and deceiver. One must undoubtedly have the teeth and claws of the lion, but princes have special need of the fox and thus of deception.

Faith means, in the first place, the keeping of one's word or being faithful to one's promises. Machiavelli uses the word in another sense: as he asks in chapter VI, how can human beings be kept firm in their beliefs? Faith has also been spoken of in connection with arms: one's arms must be kept faithful to one. The people need to keep the faith, but they cannot be relied on and are dangerously fickle. If the people are to keep the faith, the prince cannot. Peace has been made of no effect and vain by the infidelity of princes. Machiavelli seems to be ambivalent on this point. The people are fickle, and princes cannot rely on them; but princes too are fickle, and, indeed, the people are said to be more honest or decent than are the great.

The example of the infidelity of princes is that of the pope, Alexander VI, who was an effective deceiver because he knew this part of the world (and not the other?). Is Alexander in an especially good position to deceive? Does not the faith in a sense depend on him? Are not his oaths thought to be the most significant in Christendom? What of the faith that was given to the pope, the faith or pledge saying that on this rock the church would be built and the gates of hell shall not prevail against it?[1]

Machiavelli speaks repeatedly of "necessity" and of what is "necessary," most so in the paragraph in which he states how necessary it is for a prince to be merciful, faithful, human, open, and religious. The appearance of moral virtue is required by necessity; or, rather, that the prince appear to be morally virtuous is of necessity. What is even more necessary is that the prince be able to work against all the virtues in order to maintain the state.

Why the prince must appear to be morally virtuous is now stated. He must appear to be full of the five qualities listed in the previous paragraph, especially religion, because human beings judge by appearances, by the outcome or effect of a thing, not by an understanding of what is true. They look not to the causes but to the immediately perceived effects. Deception is necessary because of the lack of understanding. Human beings do not and cannot understand. If they are to obtain the good they wish, they must be deceived. They believe that they obtain the good by means of the praiseworthy qualities, but it is understanding necessity, not conformity to moral virtue, that enables one to obtain the good. Human beings insist, however, on a conformity to moral virtue, for it is the reassurance that their rulers can be trusted. They wish their rulers to act within the bounds they understand. What forces a prince to have to deceive is therefore the character of the many.

Deception is necessary, moreover, for one who is weak. Think of Odysseus and why he had to deceive. He is alone in a world full of dangers, and he must disguise himself. Machiavelli declares that in "the world there is no one but the vulgar." Those who understand are very few, and the prince cannot rule for the sake of the few. For the first time in the history of political thought, a political thinker declares in his own name that rule must be determined not by the character of the few but by that of the many. "The world" is governed not by reason but by necessity, and not by the best but by the vulgar, hence the choice for the effective truth or that which has a definite and palpable effect in the world. And Alexander VI is said to know well this part of the world.

. . .

The certainty of the sense of touch is contrasted with the deceptiveness of sight. Understanding, for Machiavelli, is truly one of comprehension or grasping, not of gazing or contemplation. Truth cannot be seen at a distance; it must be taken in hand, as fortune is to be taken in hand. One is reminded of Jean-Jacques Rousseau's description of the reliability of touch as opposed to sight, when Emile is shown how a stick looks bent when dipped in water and how he then is made to touch the stick to show that it is straight.[2]

Touch is the most important sense because it is the most certain, if not the noblest, sense. Sight was always understood to be the noblest sense of all, but now it is, according to Machiavelli, the most vulgar and deceiving sense. The principal difference between Machiavelli and the political philosophers on the question of moral virtue is in this dispute over the status of the senses. If the moral virtues are, as it were, the beautiful goddesses or "ideals" set before us, then too few of us are moved by the sight of them. To be moved by the sight of them is to suppose that a final cause can move human beings to action; that cannot happen unless it becomes an effective cause. In the world there can only be effective causes.

To live by touch and not by appearances is to give up the beautiful illusions of sight. One can always color what one finds necessary to do. Appearances deceive, but the many live by appearances and will not believe anything else. The prince must take these appearances in hand and go beyond the opinion of the people to the "effectual truth of things." One must work out a method to move beyond appearances to the true but hidden motivations of political life.

Machiavelli thus understands faith in the same way that Plato and Aristotle did. Faith is the commonly accepted belief that the way things look tells us what they are, that there is no significant division between appearance and reality. One may trust in the phenomena.

To trust the phenomena is to assume that order governs the world. Machiavelli considers that assumption to be the same as religion. The many demand the assurance of such an order, and the moral virtues are such an assurance. But that belief is a delusion that cannot govern the prince. Instead, the world is subject to the winds of fortune and the variations of things.

Does Machiavelli resort to touch, or to the manipulation of appearances, simply because of the many? If human beings could be enlightened as to the truth of their situation, it might be enough to rely on words. But one cannot rely on words; one has to turn to arms. Princes need to defend themselves, and they can do so only if they themselves come to realize their situation in the world—that there is no place for them, for there is nothing in the world but the many.

Ancient writers—the example of Achilles indicates that Machiavelli primarily means the poets—understood the nature of things but never spoke openly of the truth. Princes and poets alike, then, have known of the importance of appearances. Machiavelli, paradoxically, does not. Does he not make people doubt the intentions of the prince? Has he not made it the popular attitude to mistrust what rulers say, fostering the habit of looking for secret motivations behind the deceptive words of politicians? Machiavelli chooses to write in the vulgar tongue, and he emphasizes his departure from the usual scholastic treatise by his preservation of Latin titles. *The Prince* is obviously a vulgar work in several senses, and it is clearly meant to be such. Machiavelli explicitly informs the vulgar about how they are ruled.

One may say in response that Augustine had already made known the secret motives of princes, poets, and philosophers and was therefore suspect. What has been made evident by Augustine, and the Christian writers generally, can never be hidden again, unless all records and memories are somehow erased.

Does openness like that of Augustine depend on a providential God, that is, on Christian understanding? Only if it were true that things have an order and that a providential God sees to it that the order is maintained would it be possible to speak openly of what was previously kept from the many.

. . .

Once again Machiavelli's openness is remarkable. We have seen how the writer conceals himself behind princes; does not the writer thus practice even greater deception than the prince? We do not need to be reminded (or do we?) that Machiavelli is one of most deceptive of men; and openness, he has said, is one of the qualities the prince must never fail to show. The difficulty is that religion is said to be the most necessary quality that the prince must appear to practice, and Machiavelli has never been taken to be a religious man. On the contrary, to be Machiavel has now come to mean that one works against faith, charity, humanity, and religion.

Note that each of the three lists of praiseworthy qualities comprises five items. Four items—*pietà,* faith, humanity, and religion—appear in all the lists. Openness, charity, and integrity are each listed once. The prince may perhaps be less concerned about these.

To return, does not Machiavelli's example contradict his precepts? Or does the apparent openness (his one virtue?) about the virtues make one wonder how open he has been? Is he unable, for example, to appear religious because he is the one who establishes the new religious beliefs? He would then be the religion that all princes afterward will profess but that he himself need not. Indeed, his concealment in the new religion is necessary for its success. The question, of course, is, What is this new religion?

What Machiavelli has done is to make the people suspicious of those who rule them. This point should be understood in the light of what is said at the end of the chapter: one is to suspect present-day princes. Has he made the people at once more suspicious and more capable of being deceived? What of those who tell the people that they have been and are being deceived by their rulers? Why do they do so? Do they not seek rule, and should not one suspect their motives? What is behind the appearance of openness? If we touch the one who claims to enlighten us, what shall we come to know about him?

. . .

The most "Machiavellian" sentence of all is surely the one that appears in this chapter: "Let a prince then win and maintain the state—the means will always be judged honorable and will be praised by everyone; for the vulgar are always taken in by the appearance and outcome of a thing, and in the world there is no one but the vulgar." This sentence has been paraphrased as saying that the end justifies the means. Machiavelli does not, of course, say that. The vulgar always look to the end: they are the ones who demand success, believing that whatever is effective can only have been ordained by God. The greatest believers in the end's justifying the means are those who believe in a providential order, in which everything is finally justified by the outcome.

The prince is not to resist this tendency but to accede to it. As Machiavelli has indicated throughout these chapters on the virtues, the excellent few have to be persuaded not to indulge in the luxury of their excellence, for they cannot then do the good they wish to do. The state must above all be won and maintained, and the prince must have the opinion of the many and the majesty of the state if he is to have defenses against fortune and the variations of things.

We now have Machiavelli's most explicit statement that it is the character of the many that necessitates the prince's having to choose the effectual truth or the appearance and outcome of a thing. It may be vulgar to do so, but it has now become a well-accepted truism that there is no one in the world but the vulgar.

. . .

Finally, we are told of a "present-day prince, whom it is not good to name" and who preaches nothing but peace and faith. The reference is thought to be to Ferdinand of Aragon, but is there not another prince of peace and faith who still has imperium over men's souls? And is there a king whose name ought never be spoken? Ferdinand is unhesitatingly named in chapter XXI, where he is said to be "the first king of the Christians" in fame and glory.

NOTES

1. Matthew 16:18.
2. See the Allan Bloom edition (New York: Basic Books, 1979), 133–40, 143, 206.

CHAPTER XIX
OF AVOIDING CONTEMPT AND HATRED

In a new beginning Machiavelli summarizes the rest of the discussion of the qualities of the prince as generalities. The first and most important of these is that a prince should avoid contempt and hatred. The second is that the prince ought "to contrive that in his actions one will recognize greatness, spiritedness, gravity, strength." The third is that "his judgment be irrevocable" with respect to "the private affairs of his subjects," that is, in civil actions.

Avoiding contempt and hatred is the principal way to guard against conspiracies. The principal topic of chapter XIX is therefore how to guard against conspiracies, and it is the longest chapter in *The Prince*. The longest chapter in the *Discourses*, III.vi, is entitled "On Conspiracies." Conspiracy seems especially deserving of Machiavelli's attention.

The chapter is divided into two parts of unequal length. It opens with a summary of the rest of the qualities of the prince under the general rubric of avoiding contempt and hatred. Next comes an explanation of how a prince is to deal with the danger of conspiracy, which leads into a digression, the longest part of the chapter, about ten Roman emperors and the conspiracies against them.

. . .

Machiavelli begins by outlining that which makes a prince hated: rapaciousness and the usurpation of the goods and women of his subjects. The universality—that is, the whole world (the same as the many?)—looks especially to goods and honor. The few, in contrast, are moved by ambition, which would seem to be more than a love of their own. Their ambition is to be contrasted with the universality's love of property; the few turn out to be not as concerned with property or with benefits as are the many.

A prince becomes contemptible if he is held to be changeable, light, effeminate, pusillanimous, and irresolute in how he deals with the public and private affairs of his subjects. The prince must maintain a reputation for firmness, which is his principal defense against conspiracy. It would seem far more important for a prince not to be held in contempt than not to be hated. Machiavelli, however, proceeds to discuss at length avoiding hatred as "one of the most potent remedies a prince has for conspiracies."

The question of conspiracy is put into the context of the two fears princes must have, one from within and one from without. Good arms suffice to defend oneself against the fear that comes from outside; as for the fear that arises from within, even if external things are in motion, or in turmoil, one need not falter, as Nabis the Spartan did not. Nabis, the prince who destroyed the Spartan oligarchy, was assassinated in a conspiracy. He did not stand up to every attack, although he did stand against the whole of Greece and one of the most powerful Roman armies. Nabis seems to represent a double kind of assurance: that one may stand up to Greece and Rome and that no tyrant, however popular, can ever, in the end, be safe. The example of Nabis undermines what is subsequently said about how a prince defends himself against conspiracies.

A conspiracy is an attempt to overthrow a ruler. In praising Nabis, Machiavelli praises a tyrant who is able to sustain himself. He continues to reassure the tyrant in what is subsequently said of the difficulties facing conspirators. Instead of justifying conspiracy as necessary against tyrants, Machiavelli suggests a potent remedy for conspiracies.

Machiavelli does not raise the question of the justice of conspiracies; he seems to be wholly on the side of the prince. We realize, however, that a new prince is necessarily engaged in a conspiracy. The most excellent celebrated men were, after all, conspirators who did succeed.

The topic of conspiracy is surely the culmination of Machiavelli's teaching, for the establishment of new modes and orders cannot but be a conspiracy against someone who is ruling. Have we not learned how to conspire to usurp Italy, either as Louis XII attempted to do or as the Borgias did? Indeed, the desire to usurp is a natural desire; the only question, as discussed in chapter III, is whether one is able to succeed.

The classical political philosophers were as silent about conspiracy as they were about acquisition. Just as they spoke little of how to acquire, so did they say little about usurpation. In the *Politics,* Aristotle speaks of the ways in which changes of regime come about. Hatred and contempt are also said by Aristotle to be the causes that lead men to attack tyrannies. Machiavelli, however, makes hatred and contempt the causes that lead men to overthrow all princes and, indeed, all rule. The closest Aristotle comes to Machiavelli is the section in the *Politics* about how the tyrant may preserve his rule. Machiavelli, however, makes no distinction in chapter XIX between tyrannical rule and legitimate rule; the tyrant and the hereditary prince must preserve their rule or what they have acquired in the same way.

The way to keep one's own is to keep the people satisfied, which is the same as not being hated by the universality. Is Machiavelli referring to the universality of things? He seems to be addressing a would-be conspirator; the distinction between a prince and a would-be prince has been blurred before, notably in the remark made about Hiero in chapter VI that there are those who only lack a realm to rule. The prince or would-be prince is to understand that in the world there is nothing but the people, that is, nothing but matter—as was just said in chapter XVIII.

Machiavelli mentions the infinite difficulties that conspirators must face and how few conspiracies have succeeded. In other words, conspiracies do not always fail, and the difficulties are not insuperable. The difficulty with a conspiracy is that it must be communicated to another, giving the person to whom one speaks the possibility of gaining reward by revealing the conspiracy. How is faith to be kept in such a circumstance? A conspiracy requires that faith be kept while it is being broken. The very meaning of a conspiracy is that one does not appear to be what one is, but faith is trust in appearances. Unless one is able to read the hearts of men, or the hidden motives of the soul, one cannot know a conspirator; but neither can a conspirator know whether his companions and friends are faithful to him. Thus one cannot conspire unless one finds either rare friends or obstinate enemies of the prince. Is there a suggestion in this chapter of how a conspirator may overcome this difficulty?

. . .

Machiavelli summarizes the difficulties that confront a conspiracy, especially one against a prince who has popular goodwill. Against such a prince, it would seem most impracticable to conspire. One example is given out of an "infinite" number of conspiracies, a recent one concerning the Bentivogli, the ruling house of

Bologna. The Canneschi killed all the Bentivogli except for Giovanni, a child in swaddling clothes. The people are said to have risen up—spontaneously, it would seem—taking revenge by killing all the Canneschi. Unable to find any of the Bentivogli who were of age to rule, the people had to turn to someone in Florence who had previously been thought to be the son of a blacksmith, who then ruled the city until Giovanni was of age.

The people, it seems, have a deep longing for someone of the blood, of the family line, to which they are accustomed. In chapter II the natural prince is said to be always able to maintain himself in his state; and we have also seen that provinces like those of France cannot be conquered without first extinguishing the ancient bloodline for which the people have a natural affection.

The immediate effect of the example is to confirm the hold that blood, or the ancestral, has over the people. But then one realizes that it is possible, on the basis of a likely story, to make people believe in a connection with the blood. The people evidently desire the ancestral and the customary, but that desire can be satisfied with appearances. Faith is always concerned with appearances, and everyone has an inclination to faith, for "it is given to everyone that they see."

The account of the Bentivogli also clearly implies that one can depend on the people to rescue a prince. But we were previously told the opposite—that the people will not and cannot of themselves rescue the prince. One is deceived if one believes that. The people, after all, receive the form; they cannot in and of themselves act, for they always require leadership. Machiavelli is surely being deceptive here in his narration.[1]

. . .

Thus chapters IX and XIX indicate what the prince may expect from the people. The people need someone of ancestral blood; they need to have their faith sustained. That need can always be provided, even if that someone appears to be of base, not royal, blood. A Machiavellian thought about similar tenuous claims to an ancestral bloodline may also occur to one. Was not Augustus as little connected to Julius Caesar as Santi was to the Bentivogli?

Machiavelli concludes that little account should be taken of conspirators. He is reassuring, perhaps especially so to a prince of ancient blood who has a strong hold on the affections of the people. And, indeed, if the prince is able not to make the great desperate and to satisfy and content the people, his state will no doubt be secure. A good prince who rules well will be secure. How true—but also how obvious.

. . .

An example is then given of a well-ordered kingdom that keeps itself safe from conspiracy. He who ordered that kingdom—we are not certain who—established a "third judge" to mediate between the great and the people. The powerful are insolent and need to be restrained; the universality fear and hate the great and need to be reassured. The ambition of the one would seem to generate fear in the other. But if we restate the conflict as one between those who wish to maintain and those who wish to acquire, we can understand that it is the great who prevent the universality from acquiring—or better, that the universality believe that the great prevent them from acquiring. The universality hate the great because the latter seek to prevent the former's acquiring what is desired, which is perceived as what is needed.

The orders of the kingdom of France did not want the king to mediate this conflict directly. The third judge is a political institution, the *parlement* (law court), behind which the king may conceal his partiality. Does the notion of a third judge replace direct mediation with an indirect one in this most fundamental of all conflicts? Having said that the French do not understand the things of the state, we now find that France is held up as an example of good institutions—but not, we see, of orders. Particular institutions in France may be good, but Machiavelli never praises French modes and orders, or the political regime itself.

The kingdom of France is a modern one that is said to understand the things of war. But the arms of France are a mixture, in part mercenary and in part its own. Curiously, this account of the arms of France occurs in a chapter (XIII) in which it is mentioned that to use mercenary arms requires the appointment of a "third person," one who is neither of one's house nor of the body of mercenaries. Hence the third judge is neither of the people nor of the great. The burdensome things are to be done by the third judge. The most striking example of that precept is in the story of Remirro de Orco. Cesare Borgia subsequently replaced this most "cruel and expeditious man" with a civil judiciary, successfully concealing himself behind his servant and the institutions he established. In order to purge the *animo* of the people, however, a spectacular public execution was required.

The prince, it is said, ought to esteem the great, but we were previously told that the prince can make or unmake them and that he has their reputation at his disposal. This "new" conclusion differs in emphasis from the previous one, that the prince must have the goodwill of the people and that they must be satisfied and made content. Now the emphasis is on esteeming the great. But is not the true concern of the prince the purgation of the hatred of the universality for the great? Perhaps the modern kingdom of France has found a new way of dealing with this sempiternal conflict.

If a king may escape blame from either the people or the great by using a third person, can a conspirator escape being revealed by communicating through a third person? How would that be possible? Think of what has been said of writing and of how Virgil used the mouth of Dido to speak. Can a writer purge the minds, or *animi,* of his readers by presenting a spectacular public execution?

. . .

Machiavelli now enters into a long digression about ten Roman emperors, because it may appear to "many" that the life and death of some Roman emperor may contradict the opinion he just stated. Who are these "many"? The reference does not seem to be to the people; it may be to the princes or would-be princes, especially because he subsequently uses the familiar *tu.* One other possibility is that the reference is to his readers. At any rate, Machiavelli suspects that the previous argument has convinced many, for it appears from the lives of certain Roman emperors that someone of "great virtue of mind" and who has lived "excellently" has nevertheless lost the imperium. Many are dubious about the reassurance that a good prince can safeguard himself by turning to the people. The efficacy of the remedy suggested by Machiavelli is doubted; it does not appear to be enough to have the popular good-will, for did not some virtuous Roman emperor finally lose the imperium? Is the question here the failure of the Roman empire to maintain itself? Machiavelli proposes to show that the causes of the ruin of these emperors is no different from those he has previously stated. But he not only will answer objections by showing the causes, he will also put in "considerations" that will be notable for the one who has read "the actions of those times."

The discussion of the qualities of Commodus, Severus, Antoninus Caracalla, and Maximinus seems to be addressed to those with a theoretical interest. The nature of these men is to be carefully considered; and, indeed, the discussion of their qualities takes up two-thirds of the digression on the Roman emperors. The actions of Marcus are discussed only in general terms; those of Severus and Maximinus are discussed in particular. Indeed, Machiavelli promises the one who examines the action of Severus in detail knowledge of the two natures of the beast necessary for the prince to imitate—the fox and the lion.

Machiavelli does not say here why he wishes to discuss this period in Roman history; nor does he make evident what the considerations are that will be valuable for one who has been a reader of ancient things.[2] If we are to take the indication that the formal or plural second person is used by Machiavelli when he addresses the reader who understands, or the true addressee of *The Prince,* then he speaks to that reader when he turns to discuss the qualities of the cruel and rapacious emperors, especially the actions of Severus.

Of the ten emperors first mentioned, only seven are actually discussed. Machiavelli declares that he does not "wish to reason" about three who were "wholly contemptible." The reader is urged to examine in detail only the actions of Severus. Machiavelli himself discusses only the actions of Severus and, oddly enough, Maximinus in some detail. Is Maximinus then not "wholly contemptible"?

These Roman emperors faced not the difficulty of the conflict between the great and the people but a third difficulty: the soldiers. What was understood to be the fundamental choice in chapter IX is now revealed to be not the only choice possible. From the very beginning, Machiavelli always seems to speak in terms of a fundamental duality. Thus states are either republics or principates, and princes are either hereditary or new. Repeatedly, however, exceptions arise, or a third possibility. In what is perhaps the key chapter on this point, chapter V, the discussion gives the impression of a fundamental choice between Sparta and Rome when in fact three ways are suggested.

A remarkable reversal of the argument now occurs. Whereas before the security against conspiracy was popular goodwill, the prince is now to see that the people may be abandoned and practiced on, robbed and oppressed, to give vent to the appetites of his soldiers. In other words, the prince and his armies may sack and plunder and be liberal with the goods of the people, exactly as he would do with any country he might conquer. The prince can be rapacious and usurp the goods of his subjects and remain safe, as long as he keeps the loyalty of his soldiers. Machiavelli says nothing of the taking of women, although Commodus is blamed for indulging the armies and making them licentious. Perhaps the taking of women is still to be avoided, although there may be an implication that they are to be treated like property. Or are we to conclude that the prince must satisfy the avarice of the soldiers, not their licentiousness?

The story of the Bentivogli served to reassure the prince of the faithfulness of the people, whose affection is with the blood of the prince, even if the heir were an infant in swaddling clothes or a bastard from another city who had been always thought to be the son of a craftsman. The story was meant to confirm the warning of how difficult it is to engage in a conspiracy. So great are the difficulties that it is "impossible" that anyone would be so bold as to conspire.

The subsequent example of the kingdom of France shows, however, that the king does not depend on popular goodwill. He favors neither the people nor the great, and he seeks not the security of the people but his own. It is the first indication of the possibility that the prince need not always depend on the favor of the people.

. . .

We now discover that one need not pay any attention to the people. What may cause a conspirator to falter—the hold of that ancient blood on the people—is now set aside. The greatest security that a natural prince presumably has is no security at all against someone like Severus, who knows so well how to use the natures of the fox and the lion.

New princes who need extraordinary favors must especially turn to the soldiers. The people may be capable only of the ordinary. But the choice of the soldiers turned out to be useful or not, depending on how the emperor is able to maintain his reputation. Indeed, the success of the emperors appears to depend entirely on their reputation, which was maintained either by nature or by art.

Machiavelli explicitly declares that princes cannot escape being hated. The only question is avoiding the hatred of the powerful bodies. The people are not the only body or *università*—the prince need turn not to the *universalità* but to a *università*, or some corporation or estate in society; but he will approach it only if he is in need of the extraordinary. The Roman emperors, unlike the French king, show their partiality.

Two sets of emperors are now discussed: those who were just and humane, and those who were exceedingly cruel and rapacious. One of each set, Marcus the philosopher and Severus, comes to a good end. In his discussion, Machiavelli does not follow chronological order but discusses the members of each set, with those who came to a good end first. Thus the actions of Marcus are discussed before those of Pertinax; those of Severus are discussed before those of Commodus. Neither good qualities nor bad ones and neither good works nor evil ones suffice to maintain one's reputation. Hatred may be fomented as much by justice as by rapacity and cruelty. Nevertheless, these qualities may make one venerated or revered. That depends on the *università* whose support one needs and whose humor must therefore be followed, especially if it has become corrupt.

Justice is mentioned for the first time as among the qualities a prince might have. But the rapacious prince, Severus, appears to be as good a prince as, if not better than, Marcus. However, Machiavelli never says of either Marcus or Severus that he ought to be imitated. When the actions of Cesare are summed up, Machiavelli declares that his actions should be imitated. What is said of Marcus and Severus is that it is not necessary to follow them; they are most definitely not to be imitated. Instead, one must pick and choose certain parts.

Rome, after all, is no longer a republic. The conflict between the senate and the people has been replaced by the rule of the prince and his soldiers. That rule is a cruel one, under which the people are plundered as the mercenaries have plundered Italy. Are we not to think of the description of mercenary arms in chapter XV and wonder whether the beginning of the rule of Italy by mercenary armies began in this period? Severus acts no differently from any mercenary captain, and Francesco Sforza especially comes to mind. Both, however, failed to maintain the succession. A cruel and bestial son succeeds each one, and each is conspired against and killed.

Religion and faith are not mentioned as qualities of the emperors. Because all emperors must satisfy the soldiers, there is no need to follow the precept mentioned before, that the prince must especially show himself to be religious. The prince need not appear to have the commonly accepted moral qualities; rather, he needs only those qualities attributed to Agathocles, who is said to have led a wicked life at every stage. The prince can be without faith, without pity, and without religion yet have greatness of mind and high intentions. The reputation of the prince depends on his exhibiting not moral virtue but the virtues that permit him to acquire imperium. None of the moral virtues is crucial to his success. The only virtue that counts is the one that gives him the capacity to make good use of the natures of the fox and the lion, or the natures of the beast. We hear only of the good use of the nature of the beast by Severus, which suffices to astonish and to stupefy the soldiers and to make the people reverent and satisfied. What virtues Marcus had that made him venerated by his soldiers are not specifically mentioned. Must he not have had the virtues attributed to Agathocles and Severus?

The third way of the Roman emperors is thus to abandon all morality. We are here confronted most fully with the harsh things, with the brutal cruelty and inhumanity of the great founders and those who are like them. The princes who maintain themselves must act as Severus did and, therefore, as Agathocles did. But Cyrus, Caesar, and Alexander were rapacious, and being religious never is attributed to Cyrus. Hannibal's inhuman cruelty is praised as the cause of his being venerated, as Marcus is also venerated. Because there is no difference between Moses and Cyrus, one must assume that there is no difference in the natures of these men.

. . .

Good men and bad men alike succeed or fail; their morality or lack of it is of no consequence. If they have the virtue of Agathocles "in entering into and escaping from dangers," and his greatness of *animo,* they will always be saved. In not having to concern themselves with morality, they also do not have to concern themselves with the people. Finally, the question of heredity, or of being of ancient blood, is equally irrelevant. Agathocles rose from a low and abject station, the son of a potter, yet he was never conspired against. One must consider the obverse side of this point: the blood can also be made despicable and a cause of conspiracy, as occurred with Commodus.

The assassinations of Antoninus Caracalla, Commodus, and Maximinus are attributed to their excessive cruelty and bestiality. They have nothing in them of the man or, even more to the point, of the fox. Only Severus knew how to deceive and to color his actions. Moreover, Commodus and Maximinus made themselves contemptible; that is, they did not use cruelty well, and cruelty well used is man's only salvation.

. . .

Machiavelli tries to reassure the prince. Any prince may be killed by someone whose *animo* is so obstinate in its purpose that he does not care about death. Such obstinate minds are extremely rare, however. What the prince must guard against is doing grave injury to those in his service. Machiavelli seems as much interested in protecting the prince's servants as he is in protecting the prince. If the prince refrains from harming his servants, he himself will not be harmed. A man who knows so much about conspiracies must, of course, himself become suspect to the prince, and we have seen Machiavelli seeking throughout to prove his loyalty to the prince. Nevertheless, the possibility of an obstinate mind exists, as obstinate perhaps as a city that never forgets the name of liberty or its ancient order.

The account of the wickedness of these emperors raises two thoughts that are more important than any precepts regarding cruelty well used: we now see what has replaced the republic and that base blood can finally be made despicable in the eyes of everyone. Why is so much made of the base origins of Maximinus when the baseness of Agathocles was never a difficulty? Machiavelli seems to be reassuring the "many" of whom he spoke at the beginning of the digression that the rule of someone lowborn and who does not know how to use cruelty well cannot long continue. The whole world will finally rise against such a one.

. . .

The narration of the actions of the emperors concludes with Maximinus. Machiavelli completes the discourse with the observation that modern princes have no need to imitate the Roman emperors, for there is no necessity to satisfy the soldiers. The modern prince must instead satisfy the people. We have one more reason, then, why the Roman emperors are not to be imitated.

Only the Turk, the caliphate, and the Christian pontificate depend on soldiers.

Machiavelli declares that the Christian pontificate is similar to the caliphate, but only in terms of being neither hereditary nor new; the comparison, however, is clearly made in the context of their both being principates that must satisfy the soldiers and not the people.

The explicit connection made between the Turk and the Christian pontificate makes evident that it is the same as the kingdom of Darius or of Cyrus. Must we not then look again at every reference to the Turk in terms of the Christian pontificate? If the Turk is a prince at the head of an army, so too must be Darius and therefore Cyrus. And so too is the pontiff a prince at the head of an army composed of many nations and of infinite races.

One must also conclude that the Roman emperors ruled like the Turk. That would mean that the victory of Severus is the triumph of Turkish rule or the kingdom of Darius. We have seen how the reasoning about Moses is replaced by the reasoning about Cyrus. May not *The Prince* as a whole be thought of as a reasoning about Cyrus?

. . .

Machiavelli returns from the digression to the matter at hand. He has reassured us about conspiracies, whether we wish to guard against them or are thinking of attempting one. His mode of writing permits him to discourse on a matter while dealing with other considerations. He repeats his point regarding hatred or disdain as the cause of the overthrow of rulers. We are supposed to know now why no mode of procedure, whether cruel and bestial or kindly and human, is safe. In fact, we have come to see the criminal nature of the founder.

Chapter XIX brings to a conclusion, then, the discourse begun in chapter XV. The discussion of the qualities of the prince turned out to be a discussion of the nature of the people and what the prince is forced to do by necessity. Chapter XIX is the fullest explication of what that necessity signifies.

In this connection, can the distinction between Severus the founder and Marcus the preserver be maintained? We have seen that the prince has to "think of a mode" that would remind his subjects of their need of the state and of him. Men willingly change masters, and the people have to be made to believe by force, for there will always come a time when they will no longer believe and must therefore be kept in fear. To keep men in fear is to keep them reminded of the founding and the orders that were established. It would seem that rulers must, in effect, always be founders, for in maintaining they will have to enter into and escape from dangers, stand up to and overcome adverse things, and make many spirited and dangerous decisions. How different, then, can the actions of one who seeks to maintain be from one who seeks to acquire?

NOTES

1. One need only compare Machiavelli's account of this incident in the *Florentine Histories* (VI.9–10) to see how misleading he has been. At the time of the assassinations Giovanni was six years old, not a babe in swaddling clothes. The city commissioners led the counterattack on the Canneschi; it was not a spontaneous

uprising by the people. The cause of the search for someone of the Bentivogli line to rule was due to fear on the part of the Bentivogli faction that divisions might otherwise occur; and one man, the count of Poppi, suggests that he knows of a descendant of Annibale. Moreover, the son of the blacksmith turns out to be a wool worker, one of the lowest of the people or a plebeian, one of the very same workers whom Giorgio Scali led in the Tumult of the Ciompi (1378). Thus a base-born bastard governs the city until the true scion of the house is able to rule. And all this was possible because of popular goodwill.

2. But in the *Discourses* I.10 he tells us that the reign of Marcus Aurelius was the close of the golden age of the Roman Empire. The period with which chapter XIX is concerned is therefore that which follows the best age of the empire, one in which "the world" was no longer triumphant.

PART FOUR

OF THE PRUDENCE OF THE PRINCE

IF FORTRESSES AND MANY OTHER THINGS WHICH EVERY-
DAY ARE EMPLOYED BY PRINCES ARE USEFUL OR USELESS

The topic of the chapter is what princes have made and done in order to keep the state secure. We are given a set of things made or done, ten in all: five in chapter XX and five in chapter XXI. The question asked is whether these things are useful or useless; Machiavelli indicates that the answer cannot be definite because one must consider the particulars of every case. He will, however, discuss them as generally as the matter will permit. (The most frequent use of the word *matter* occurs in chapters XIX and XX.) But why does he consider it important to speak of these things generally when he knows that, because they are concerned with particulars, they ought to be left to the prudence of the prince? How useful or useless is the advice he gives?

The chapter is in fact the beginning of a new division of the argument on the prudence of the prince, which comprises chapters XX through XXIII. Prudence is concerned with particulars, so the question we have asked is even more to the point. Why does Machiavelli attempt to give rules for a matter he knows cannot be generalized? The simplest answer is that somehow these things can no longer be left to prudence, or that prudence is lacking. General precepts would seem to be useless to everyone, however: the prudent do not need them, and the imprudent will not be made prudent by maxims. Nonetheless, Machiavelli will consider these things; he will continue on his way despite all reason and experience.

He begins by mentioning five things employed by some princes to keep the state secure, each of which he then discusses: the subjects are disarmed; the subject towns are divided into factions; the prince imitates fortune and acts as an agent provocateur, deliberately stirring up enmities in order to crush them; the new prince makes use of men who were opposed to him; and fortresses are built or destroyed. In the subsequent discussion he advocates in his own name the ordering of arms and the use of suspected men. He is especially emphatic that suspected men ought to be used by the prince, a precept that is of particular interest to Machiavelli. He also praises the building of fortresses because the ancients used them, although they have proved to be useless, as he writes, "in our times." He appears undecided about the question, but if war is to be made against foreigners and not the people, then fortresses ought not to be built. Factions are rejected outright as being useless in war, and because a prince must always be prepared for war, factions are simply useless. As for nourishing enmities, Machiavelli makes no comment; he merely repeats the judgment of "many" and does not say whether that judgment is right.

. . .

Machiavelli declares, first of all, that no new prince has ever disarmed his sub-jects. Indeed, if the subjects are disarmed, the prince must arm them. Arms and faith are linked once again: for men to be faithful, they must be armed, but armed in one's own mode, so they become one's own arms. In other words, we are putting into practice what was written in chapters III and XII. We are to review, as it were, the precepts of the handbook for princes.

One disarms only the subjects of a new state that is added to an old one. But what is now suggested, that only those who were one's own soldiers in the old state be employed in the newly acquired state, sounds very much like establishing gar-risons, a policy that was said to be useless and harmful. Instead of soldiers, the prince was previously advised either to establish colonies or to live in the new do-minion himself. We must ask whether ordering one's own arms does not mean arm-ing the people? What can he mean by suggesting that the new state must be dis-armed and made soft and effeminate?

The suspicion is now confirmed that Machiavelli has something in mind other than listing useless maxims. One cannot escape the feeling that one is being sub-jected to an examination to see whether or not one has been paying attention. No doubt Machiavelli is also amusing himself.

The prince has to order his own arms; that has been said repeatedly. The pre-cept, as do all general maxims, has a truth in it. But the difficulty lies in know-ing not the precept, which everyone knows, but what one is to do in a given cir-cumstance.

. . .

Machiavelli now speaks of "our"—that is, Florentine—ancestors and old men who hold to the maxim that Pistoia should be held with factions and Pisa with fortresses. Such a maxim is "ours," and it has the authority of long experience. What is immediately discussed are not fortresses but factions; and we are reminded that the belief in the efficacy of factions arises from the previous state of affairs in Italy, when the five principal powers kept a balance with one another and preserved the peace. The entrance of Charles VIII disturbed this balance, as was described in chapter XI, where the word *faction* was used six times. We are made once again to reflect on the situation in Italy.

The balance of the powers in Italy and the tranquillity that resulted made fac-tions useful because they kept the subject cities internally divided and thus unable to defend themselves. Modern republics, rather than the ancient republics, are the ones that seem to make use of factions, for the examples given are Florence and Venice. The precept is thus a modern, not an ancient, one; it is "ours." However, Machiavelli finally concludes that factions never do anyone any good, which means that the Florentine ancestors and old men are wholly mistaken, for in no instance is such a policy good.

The specific factions that divided the subject cities of Florence and Venice were the Guelf and Ghibbeline "sects." Moved by the reasons mentioned in the previous paragraph, Venetians especially tried to foster these factions. Are sects factions? Or, rather, are modern factions in truth sects? The division between the Guelfs and the Ghibbelines first signifies the division between the adherents of the pope (Guelf) and those of the emperor (Ghibbeline). But the names were subsequently attached to the popular (Ghibbeline) and oligarchic (Guelfs) factions in the Italian cities, especially in Florence.

Both the papal claims and the imperial claims are universal in extent; the question at issue is whether the jurisdiction of the emperor in the temporal realm is to be exercised independently of the papacy. The connection of mercenary arms with the papal and imperial struggle is indicated in chapter XII of *The Prince*. The anti-imperial struggle brought the church and the cities into an alliance, and, because these had no experience of arms, they hired foreign soldiers. Mercenary arms, then, are the direct consequence of papal and popular power, which took imperium away from the emperor.

To use sectarian divisions has the consequence of disarming the city. A city cannot be divided in the most fundamental sense, in that it must pay attention to its own interests, not the claims of some outside power. That is, to use factions is to attempt to divide the faith of the citizens, making them adhere to an outside power. Such a division works if the outside power cannot intervene; but if it can intervene, then the weakened city will always fall. Only when the church gains temporal power does the weakness of the Florentine and Venetian—that is, Italian—policy show itself and the two greatest republics of Italy are unable to defend themselves. The tendency to use sects is apparently a republican one, and it is one that destroys republics. The question of the unity of republics is one of arms.

. . .

The counsel that a prince should make difficulties for himself, so that he may increase his greatness by overcoming them, suggests that fortune may not provide sufficient difficulties for a new prince to test his virtue. Given the previous discussion of all the difficulties a new prince has to confront, it would seem that this would be most unlikely. Fortune, however, may not provide an occasion for one of a princely nature. If all is settled and there appears to be no way whereby he can become the lord of a state, should he make enemies for oneself? Did not Alexander VI deliberately make enemies when he consented to the French invasion of Italy? But does not being a new prince necessarily make for enemies? Is this not again superfluous advice? If one is to be a new prince, one will nourish enmities; there is no need to wait for fortune.

What is being suggested is that the prince imitate the actions of fortune. What is implied is that the world is so ordered that the natural tendency is for everything to remain at rest. A prince thus has to imitate fortune in order to make his own opportunities or occasions. But if everything is in motion or in constant change, there would seem to be no need to imitate fortune.

. . .

As for making use of suspect men—that is, those who were loyal to the previous regime—one understands Machiavelli's need to reassure a prince that such men can be useful and trusted. Machiavelli was a minister in the Florentine republic and had opposed the Medicis. He now wishes to gain the favor of the Medici house. He faces the further difficulty, however, that writers of handbooks for princes are always suspect. Does the writer know more than the prince? If he knows how to rule, why does he not want to rule, because that is surely what everyone should desire? If he does not know how to rule, is not his advice useless? Indeed, why should a prince who knows how to rule concern himself with writers in the first place? Would not the only reason be that writers may be dangerous to him? We are reminded of the explanation Machiavelli offers in the Epistle Dedicatory that it is one thing to know the nature of princes and another to know the nature of the people. But we know that he who rules must understand all the natures and that the writers are the ones who provide the matter for the exercise of the body and mind of the prince.

The "matter" of Machiavelli, in one of its principal meanings, is the argument he has been pursuing. He has spoken of the variety of "matter" in his work, of the "matter" he has been disputing, and he proposes to return to his "matter." But "matter" has also meant the material, the potency into which form is introduced and the occasion or opportunity for receiving form. Both meanings have been used in chapter XX. Is not his work—the text itself—"matter" in both senses of the word? Should not *The Prince* be considered "matter" in both senses? The text itself is the stuff to which form has been given: it is the "occasion" spoken of in chapter VI, and it therefore is an imitation of fortune, but, unlike fortune, it is ruled by the form of the writer's *animo*. The text also provides matter in that it provides the stuff for the exercise of the body. Here are the hills and valleys, the rivers and marshes, and, indeed, all the natures both of the sites and of human beings.

Does matter have an order that stays the same? If so, one could use men contented with the former state. But if there is no such order in matter, no one and nothing can be trusted by the prince, neither those whom he supposes to be his friends nor those whom he supposes to be his enemies. Again, a wise prince would know this. An unwise prince might be persuaded to consider employing Machiavelli. Men may be suspected, but the writer cannot, for he gives the stuff or occasion or matter that supports the prince.

Is writing thus the most enduring of formed matter? Can a writer trust and have friends in a way that a prince cannot? And what of the advice itself? The prince is to use those men who are content with things as they are, who do not seek change. All men, however, seek change and are therefore suspect, so one cannot make such a distinction as is made here. Men are as variable as matter is. Is it not the writer who can especially use such men? These suspect men remind one of the way in which philosophers have been characterized: the philosophers may be said to be content with things as they are because they understand the cosmos, the order of things, as eternal. They can be thought of as optimists, believing that things are ordered as well as they can possibly be; hence they are, by definition, content.

. . .

Fortresses are the refuge of princes and have been used since antiquity. "In our times," however, princes find them useless. The first conclusion, then, is that fortresses are useful or not, depending on the times.

The further discussion of the point is addressed to a prince, not to a republic. All the examples in this account of fortresses are of princes, for to use a fortress is not to trust the people. The choice is between fortresses and the people.

A fortress is used by those, we recall from chapter X, who cannot put an army into the field and encounter the enemy in open battle. That means that one is dependent on others, or that one is like a woman. And only a woman, the countess of Forlì, benefited from a fortress, having outside help come to her rescue. In the end, however, the countess was assaulted by Cesare—the imagery of rape seems to be suggested here.

Machiavelli presents the weakness of fortresses here in terms of their vulnerability to popular rebellions and foreign intervention. One needs the people, of course, for if a prince is to be self-sufficient he must have an armed and self-sufficient people. If the prince who uses fortresses is dependent on foreign powers, so are the people. And if the people can be oppressed by a prince and a foreigner, so too can a prince be endangered by a foreigner. Such a prince and such a people are in the same situation as was the countess of Forlì: they wait to be assaulted by a Cesare.

One notices that Cesare Borgia is here thought of as a foreigner. The context is ambiguous. Is he a foreigner to Italy simply, or only a foreigner to Forlì?

The praise of the German cities should not be forgotten. Despite their use of fortresses, these republics (and not principates, therefore) maintain the ancient military exercises and are able to withstand long sieges. Machiavelli has given an assurance in chapter X that a powerful, spirited, and prudent prince will always be able to hold firm the minds of the citizens and thus will always be able to hold out against the enemy. What is said of fortresses in chapter X seems to suggest that one can have both a fortress and the support of the people. These are not necessarily opposed to one another, as he seems to suggest with his example of the Castle of Milan.

Here we are told that fortresses are simply useless. We discover that to rely on fortresses is not to rely on the people. What a prince ought to do is to see to it that he is not hated by the people: for him, that will be "the best fortress there is." To build a fortress is not to trust or to depend on the people; in terms of chapter IX, it is to choose the great instead of the people. The ancient philosophers would have dwelt in fortresses, for they chose the great and not the people. The strength of a principate depends wholly on the prince's relationship with the people. If he has the people with him, he will be able to put an army in the field and will require no fortresses. A prince who relies on fortresses fears the people rather than foreigners. We must suppose, then, that Machiavelli fears the foreign power more than he does the people.

Is not a fortress an attempt to fix an order? Fortresses are used by those who believe that there is an unchanging, fundamental order to things. Is it the reflection or symbol of the belief that there is a fixed hierarchical order in the universe? The issue is how one understands the nature of things and the difference between a reliance on prudence rather than on precepts. Is a reliance on precepts the consequence of believing in a fixed order of the universe?

Fortresses are useful, we are now told, according to the "times," and "times" may refer to circumstances as well as to historical periods. The circumstances of the German cities may be such that fortresses are useful to them in a way that they are not useful in Italy. One different circumstance may be that ancient military orders are in Germany but not in Italy.

Nevertheless, the German cities are not self-sufficient. The fact remains that they cannot put an army into the field. They can stand up to the emperor, but that is because the emperor is the weakest of all temporal princes. Moreover, if the emperor is a weak prince, must not one conclude that there is another prince on whom he depends? And has it not been suggested that this prince has turned to his soldiers and does not concern himself with the people? Is he not, then, also dependent, and does he, in turn, also use fortresses? Cannot this latter principate be called "a mighty fortress"?

Thus factions and fortresses are connected to one another, in that both indicate a dependence and a vulnerability to foreign powers and hence a weakness with respect to war. To have divided loyalties is to have factions, and a foreign power can especially make use of factions. To rely on fortresses signifies that one fears the people more than foreigners; it is not to be properly armed; it is, indeed, the consequence of depending on others, especially foreign powers. One may even say that to choose to build a fortress is to choose to rely on an outside power, the consequence of which we have seen in chapter XIII.

Machiavelli does speak of factions and fortresses together in the precept advanced by the Florentine ancestors and old men and by those esteemed as wise. The temptation to use factions seems to be especially popular: the use of fortresses arises from a fear of the people. Fortresses are also ancient, and Machiavelli condemns the use of factions and praises the use of fortresses, if they can be built without neglecting the people and incurring their hatred. He does not praise the Florentine tradition, but he does praise fortresses as an antique mode. The Florentine ancestors do not seem, therefore, to be sufficiently antique. The most puzzling question concerns the assurance given that a prince can use a fortress to sustain a long siege, when at the same time it is said that an armed people is the best fortress. The modes of ordering arms to which he wholly gives himself would seem to be the true fortresses.

CHAPTER XXI

WHAT A PRINCE SHOULD DO THAT HE MAY BE ESTEEMED

The next five precepts begin with the prince's giving of "rare examples," by which is meant that the examples contain actions that will astonish and stupefy. These actions are to be given with respect to both external and internal things. The seventh precept is that a prince is to be a true friend and a true enemy, or that a prince is not to be neutral. The discussion of this precept takes up the greater part of the chapter. Then, under what seems to be one heading, Machiavelli concludes by saying that the prince should be a lover of virtue and should honor the excellent in an art; that he should encourage his subjects to pursue their mercantile and agricultural activities as well as other trades; and that he should keep the people busy with feasts and spectacles at the proper times of the year. Having begun with arms, he ends with a picture of peace, prosperity, and pleasure. In the end, these precepts seem to concern the effects that a prudent prince may have.

. . .

The princes who represent rare examples are King Ferdinand of Aragon and Duke Bernabò Visconti of Milan. No ancient examples are given, so perhaps all rare examples are modern. The reader with a theoretical interest is now asked to consider the actions of Ferdinand, which are said to be extremely great and in some cases extraordinary. The reader is called on to think through such actions.

The successful siege of Granada appears to be one of Ferdinand's great actions, along with the attacks on Africa, Italy, and France. The rare example, however, is the expulsion of the Marranos, which is said to be miserable, or the opposite of great. But if a rare example is wretched, can it nonetheless be called extraordinary? A rare example is clearly one that is unimaginable to most men. Men are thrilled by these spectacularly unexpected actions, and they are not only stupefied but also satisfied.

Ferdinand is called "the first king of the Christians," and the rarest and most miserable of his actions arises out of a pious cruelty, which is to be distinguished, it would seem, from cruelty well used; for cruelty well used is not miserable but a remedy for one's state with God and men. The modern or Christian king inflicts a wretched or useless cruelty. One would think that to inflict such useless cruelty is the greatest of the sins of princes, for it does not lead to salvation. It therefore leads to damnation, and one may ask what Machiavellian damnation would be.

To understand why pious cruelty is useless, one should consider that the expulsion of the Marranos was the consequence of a mistrust of the outward conversion of the Spanish Jews, for the inward conversion could not be known.[1] No outward sign of conversion, not even, for example, the eating of pork, could suffice. The pious cruelty would thus seem to be the demand that the inward disposition of the soul be known. Is this why his action is so rare or extraordinary, that is, beyond the merely human?

One must begin to doubt the usefulness of the actions of such princes as Ferdinand. Bernabò of Milan is also said to have rewarded and punished extraordinarily those who did extraordinary things. But we have seen that the useful is the natural and the ordinary. And nothing is said about extraordinary deeds and rewards in the last paragraph of the chapter.

The importance of the effect of the extraordinary on the people is something the moderns seem to know better than do the ancients. If useful cruelty is to be distinguished from pious cruelty, then perhaps the former does not have the spectacular quality of the latter. The reputation to be gained by extraordinary actions is that of greatness and excellent ingenuity. The reputation is not that of prudence; and we have seen how dubious greatness is, for it can arise from fortune rather than from virtue.

. . .

The prince is counseled to be open in his friendships and enmities and not to be neutral. Such openness is always more useful; for a prince to have friends he must openly be a friend. Machiavelli gives a quotation in Latin, one he has adapted from Livy, about the Roman legate who warns the Achaeans that to be neutral is to be delivered into the hands of the victors, for whoever wins will treat them as enemies.

The Roman legate in question was Titus Quintius Flamininus, whose life Plutarch chooses as the parallel to Philopoemen's life. The passage quoted concludes the reply Titus Quintius makes to the ambassador of Antiochus, who is described as a boaster. Quintius begins his reply by saying that Antiochus and the Aetolians filled one another's minds with groundless hopes through lies and boasts of strength they did not possess. Quintius compares the situation to a dinner given by his friend in Chalcis, who served game of great variety at the summer solstice, when game was out of season. The host admitted that all the great variety of game was, in fact, made out of tame swine by means of different seasonings. So too, said Quintius, were the forces and weapons of Antiochus all the same kind, simply tame pork dressed up in various guises: they were all Syrian and all of a slavish disposition and unable to fight. The great king of Syria, Antiochus, was in fact a beggar, without forces, food, or money. Thus the Aetolians should trust not in the great king but in the Romans, whose capacity to protect was tried and known.

The argument against neutrality made by Titus is in terms of rejecting the overtures of an Asiatic king who boasts of the innumerable peoples he has collected into an army but whose power is based on words and vain hopes. One should instead choose the certain and known power of the Romans. One is reminded, further, that in Plutarch's *Lives* the question is raised of whether Titus or Philopoemen is the more praiseworthy. Titus should be praised for the gentleness and philanthropy he showed in granting liberty to the Greeks, but Philopoemen is praised for opposing the Romans, despite the fact that they were more powerful. Plutarch concludes that it is far more difficult to oppose someone more powerful than it is to grant favors to suppliants. We are thus reminded that the Romans never took the middle way, and neutrality is the middle way between enmity and friendship.

The argument against neutrality is now stated in terms of the obligations and the "contract of love" that are established through open friendship. No one—or, rather, no powerful one—it is said, will be so ungrateful that he will forget such obligations. Are we to think of all possible contracts of love with a powerful one? Is not *covenant* another word for a contract? Is the teaching here that one should boldly disclose himself to be on one side or the other? And whoever the victor is, he has to have some respect for justice; that is, he must fear that he may lose in the future and would wish to be treated with justice.

Having heard of human fickleness and ingratitude, of their wickedness and consequent lack of faithfulness, and of the need for cruelty and fear, one is surprised at the importance given to the feelings of obligation, gratitude, love, and justice that are now said to make men have respect. The mention of justice is especially striking, for it has been mentioned only once before and is never mentioned again. The only other mention of justice concerned the virtuous Roman emperors, all of whom, except for Marcus Aurelius, came to a sad end. Justice was not a virtue that proved useful to them. What proved useful were the qualities of the fox and the lion, or deception and cruelty. And the first king of the Christians is especially known for his capacity for rare examples and pious cruelty. One should also remember that Alexander VI was known for his capacity to deceive.

Machiavelli seeks to prove that resolute action is preferable to neutrality in every instance. The first possibility he presents is that one allies oneself to a greater power, which would be even greater after its victory. That clearly means that one is going to be even more at the mercy of such a power after a victory. Louis XII, it was said, made the mistake of destroying the weaker powers in Italy, thereby strengthening the powerful. Why would a prince wish to go to the aid of a power greater than his?

Nonetheless, if a prince does turn to a greater power, he can rely on the conqueror's love, honesty, gratitude, and respect for justice. One can scarcely believe that Machiavelli can now say this in all apparent sincerity. What kind of mocking preceptor have we here before us? For is this not, indeed, mockery? If we are deceived, are we not mocked? But if we are not, then an even more wicked thought may come to us: how much can one depend on any contract of love? Machiavelli has not led us to depend on the love and the justice of human beings, especially of rulers. What then of the love and the justice of other powers?

When one loses, one is attached to a fortune that can win again. That possibility also depends on a respect for justice. The reference to fortune makes one wonder whether fortune rewards virtue. It would seem that the more the world is governed by fortune, the less one can depend on love and justice. One need not be concerned about loss if not fortune but some kind of providential order governs, because that order would then provide the necessary support for justice, gratitude, honesty, and love. The question then is how much "the matter in itself" may support, or how much the matter is formed and ordered by a providential God.

The second case is where the opponents are both powers weaker than oneself.

Now, Machiavelli declares, it is most prudent to be wholly a friend of one side. One is then in the reverse of the previous situation, for one is now the stronger power and can only profit from the destruction of the other power. Open friendship is prudent if one's ally is weaker than one.

Machiavelli now answers the question about why a prince would ever ally with a stronger power. A prince should never do so, except when constrained by necessity, for a prince should never leave himself at the discretion of another. Necessity does not permit the prince to be wholly a friend or an enemy: neutrality would seem to be the wisest policy to follow, as the Venetians should have done in the war between France and the duke of Milan. To be neutral or to follow the middle way (not to be wholly a friend or wholly an enemy) is now the prudent part, and in advocating neutrality Machiavelli abandons the Roman way of never being neutral. We again come to a Machiavellian third way, which is not Roman and which is the prudent way. Let us understand, to repeat, that Machiavelli counsels neutrality especially with respect to relationships with one who is more powerful. Or we may put the question another way: neutral to whom? To the greatest power that is believed to exist?

The final statement is that no part is safe; that is, no general rule can be followed. Instead, the state must exercise prudence and must choose the less bad as the good. Here, for the first time, a state is said to act. Not a prince but his state must pick the less bad as the good. Does this indicate that it is the prince's state that must make this kind of choice? For a state there can be no good choices. But can a prince be distinguished from his state?

To pick the less bad as the good is to disagree with Aristotle that the mean is the good. So powerful is the rule of necessity that there is nothing that can simply be called good; there is only the less evil. Thus there can be no best regime, perhaps not even the odor of it. What is evident, however, is that a resolute course of action is not safe and that one may be forced into neutrality as the least of evils. Prudence is the recognition that necessity may constrain one not to be bold. The conclusion one might have expected—that necessity constrains one to be bold—is reversed. But surely we have been prepared for this most Machiavellian of conclusions.

. . .

The peace, quiet, and prosperity that should be the consequence of the good rule of the prince is in sharp contrast to the description of Ferdinand and his actions at the beginning of the chapter. Rare examples keep the minds of the citizens in suspense and wonder as they await the next thrilling action of the prince. According to the final paragraph of the chapter, however, the citizens should be permitted to practice their trades quietly and to be secure in their possessions and lives. Is there not an emphasis here on gaining the esteem of the people through the maintenance of appearances? Machiavelli has previously noted that cruel measures ought to be carried out early and at one stroke and not repeated. That would be cruelty well used. The actions of Ferdinand and Bernabò are not apt to quiet men's minds and to make them secure. The pious cruelty of Ferdinand is not the cruelty well used of Agathocles and others. Moreover, the natural prince proceeds in such a way that changes are not noticed but appear to be continuous with ancestral orders. In other words, the natural prince proceeds in such a way that there are no disturbances of the public mind, no scandals. These are the appearances that must be preserved. What is preserved is the appearance of an order that flows on in an expected and customary cycle. Such is especially suggested by the prince's concern with celebrating feasts and spectacles "at the proper times of the year." Which of these precepts is the prince to follow, the sixth or the last three? Is not the answer suggested that the prince must be prudent and learn how to choose? The suspicion is further confirmed that we are engaged in an exercise in which the prudence of the reader is being tested. One thinks of a military training area full of booby traps, making one wonder whether one has escaped them or whether they have been unwittingly and ignorantly set off, leaving a mark perceived only by the prudent.

. . .

The true counsel in chapters XX and XXI concerns the relationships of the earthly prince with the spiritual kingdom, or the kingdom of God. The first set of five precepts centers on the question of whether the new prince should order himself in imitation of the kingdom of God. To put it another way, does the earthly prince have to introduce factions and to build fortresses? Does he have to imitate fortune because otherwise all things are provided for?

The second set of precepts contrasts what would have to be called the policies of the spiritual order, or perhaps the ecclesiastical principate, with those of the prudent prince. The contrast can also be described in two other ways: as that between the extraordinary and rare examples on the one hand and the natural and ordinary on the other hand; and as that between pious cruelty and useful cruelty.

NOTE

1. The name *Marrano,* meaning swine, was given in contempt by the Spanish and Portuguese to the converted Jews, presumably because they ate pork.

CHAPTER XXII

OF THOSE WHOM PRINCES HAVE AS SECRETARIES

The prudence of the prince is now explicitly the topic. Prudence was the implicit topic before, but it was never so stated. Instead, the prince was given precepts to follow. Now the choice of ministers is the first specific thing said to depend on the prudence of the prince. Here the man himself is in question: not his state but his brains. The first error the prince makes, says Machiavelli, is in his choice of the men around him.

Pandolfo Petrucci was initially mentioned as an example of a prince who used men who belonged to the previous regime and had opposed him. He is now said to be a prudent prince who chose rightly in the first choice a ruler has to make: for having chosen Antonio da Venafro as his minister, Petrucci was thought to be an exceedingly worthy man. A prince may bask in the glow of his minister's virtue.

Machiavelli distinguishes "three kinds of brains." The first is capable of inventing on its own; it does not follow the path beaten by others and does not proceed, therefore, by imitations. The second must imitate, but it understands what others understand. We are not told, however, how such a brain can understand anything if it does not understand on its own. Must not the distinction between the first and the second kinds of brains have to blur? If the second kind of brain is always dependent on another, can it be said to understand anything? That would make it like the third kind of brain, which can understand nothing. We are reminded of Machiavelli's habit of dividing things into two, as he does in the first chapter. It is clear, however, that the prince must understand on his own. He must know the minister's "bad and good works."

Above all, the prince must be able to see through deceptions. But what if the minister is a cunning fox and able to deceive at will? Petrucci himself rose to the principate of Siena by deception. Would not that indicate that the prince must be more cunning than any minister?

The prince is then told of a mode that never fails. If a prince sees a minister doing things not in his interest, he should remove the minister. To use a Machiavellian phrase, that is a truth clearer than daylight, but it is also one as superfluous as a candle in bright sunlight. Indeed, this may be the clearest example of the character of chapters XX through XXIII. A prudent prince will not need any of the advice proffered, especially when the advice consists of such simpleminded statements as, "Don't use men who act against your interests."

One need only remember who Machiavelli was, and what he says in the Epistle Dedicatory, to understand the jest being made. Machiavelli is an ousted minister, the secretary of state of the republic that had been overthrown by the Medici. He seeks office from Lorenzo de' Medici, the newly installed ruler, whom he now attempts to persuade that he, Machiavelli, has the means whereby Lorenzo can come to know and to understand the nature of princes. He promises Lorenzo that he has a mode of dealing with men such as Machiavelli, who are under suspicion, that never fails. Lorenzo is assured that prudent princes have always found such men more useful. Machiavelli reminds one here of a huckster proclaiming that what he is selling has an ironclad guarantee and that the buyer has nothing whatsoever to lose. Machiavelli will be no threat to Lorenzo or the house of the Medici if he is hired by them.

We then have the cream of the jest. To continue to keep such men "good," the prince ought to honor and to enrich them, to share honors and burdens, so that the minister will never think of overthrowing so gracious and liberal a prince. Presumably such openhanded friendliness will establish a contract of love between prince and secretary, and the secretary will not be able to be dishonest and ungrateful to his prince. How does one give in such a way so that the minister's desires are not increased? Have we not heard that the desire to acquire is natural and ordinary, that men are lovers of gain, and that they forget the death of a father sooner than the loss of patrimony?

Did Machiavelli think that such advice would mislead Lorenzo? We have seen that Machiavelli regards Lorenzo as an imperceptive prince. That imperceptive prince is now given a most misleading assurance that limits can be placed on desires by indulging them to the utmost. The outcome, as is said at the end of the chapter, can only be harmful to one who cannot see through so transparent a deceit. The chapter is intended to deceive, but to deceive only the most obtuse (and perhaps in this world there is mostly the obtuse). That kind of deception is properly called flattery. And when it comes to certain princes, or certain kinds of princes, Machiavelli apparently believes in Benjamin Disraeli's dictum that flattery should be laid on "with a trowel." We ought to be amused, then, when we turn to the next chapter and find that it concerns flattery.

CHAPTER XXIII
IN WHAT MODE FLATTERERS ARE TO BE AVOIDED

Only the most prudent can defend themselves against flatterers. One always wishes to believe them, for one is always pleased with one's own. There are three modes of dealing with flattery. First, one may do nothing at all. The second is a mode that does not work. To avoid flattery the prince tries to encourage men to speak the truth freely to him. He soon discovers, however, that such liberty leads to contempt, for everyone will then think he has the right to speak to the prince as an equal, with all the attendant consequences.

A third mode, therefore, is to be followed. As one who has praised the Romans for not following the middle way, Machiavelli seems fond of the "third way," taken to avoid entrapment between two difficult choices. As usual, prudence must find an escape from a sharp dilemma. The third mode is to choose a few "wise men" who are given "free will" to speak the truth and who incur displeasure if they in any way hesitate to speak openly. But once the prince has deliberated and chosen, he is to be unyielding in his choice.

The example of Maximilian, the Holy Roman emperor, is the only one given in this short chapter. We have seen that the struggle between pope and emperor has led to the disarming of Italy. The claims of the pope in the temporal sphere have seriously weakened the emperor, so much so that he cannot govern the German cities, who are themselves so weak that they cannot put an army into the field. Thus he is the weakest of all temporal princes. That weakness is endemic, for there is an implicit divided jurisdiction both temporally and spiritually. Is the emperor the vicegerent of God on earth? With respect to temporal affairs, is the final authority the emperor's? Or must the emperor carry out the teachings of the church, whose head is the pontiff? Does God make known His plans only through His only vicegerent, the pope?

We are inevitably led to the question of the divided counsels that the emperor receives. Are we also to rethink chapter XXII in terms of what kinds of ministers the modern ruler must choose? Are there ministers who always have to think of their own interests and never that of the prince?

The divided counsels come from the division not only between the spiritual and the temporal but also between the universal and the particular, or what is one's own and what is not. We need simply ask the questions, What is the fatherland of the emperor? What is his own? The distinction between what is one's own and what is not is, of course, the distinction between the citizen and the stranger. But a Christian is always a stranger; he has no fatherland, nothing of his own here on earth. Is the Christian emperor also a stranger on earth? We might also ask whether the Christian emperor can act according to his own mode or must always act according to the mode of another. To do something according to one's own mode is especially to have one's own arms, as David, especially, did.

We are also led to wonder whether the emperor can be anything other than secretive. From whom can he take counsel? Whose counsel is he to heed? How is he to know of the plans of God for mankind as a whole, for is it not these that he must come to know? Moreover, do not these plans go beyond the earthly realm? Can there be public deliberations about the hidden purposes of providence? Revelation, by definition, is that which cannot be grasped by the unaided human mind. The working out of God's divine plan can be seen only by the eyes of faith, not by merely human eyes. Who, then, makes evident the invisible order of things to a blind and ignorant mankind? Israel was divided by the claims of king and prophet, and Christendom has been divided by the claims of emperor and pope.

. . .

Why we are to be reminded of the Holy Roman emperor in a chapter on flattery may be understood in terms of the general topic of these chapters: the prudence of the prince. The division of Christendom prevents the exercise of prudence. The lack of prudence means the domination of flattery, for if there is no deliberation, there can only be an appeal to whatever can move the prince, to his private and whimsical desires. The universality of Christianity leads to the universalization of private desire. One sees the truth of this conclusion in the sectarian divisions of Christianity, where every private interpretation of God's Word is thought of as authoritative over all mankind. That belief is, one can say, flattery of the utmost degree.

To avoid flattery one should take counsel only when one wishes and from whom one wishes. The prince is to question widely about everything and to encourage liberty of speech (and presumably of opinion) among his counselors. But the only defense against flattery is a prudent nature. The prince must himself be prudent; and Machiavelli finally states explicitly what has been implicit in these chapters. We are now told of a "general rule that never fails," which is to be distinguished from "a mode that never fails." A mode, or a way of doing things, cannot but fail, as we shall see in Chapter XXV, for when circumstances change, men find it difficult if not impossible to change their modes. A general rule, in contrast, can be applied prudently to a particular circumstance.

An imprudent prince cannot save himself unless he gives himself wholly over to a "most prudent man." The word used here, *rimettersi,* was used only once before, at the end of chapter XIII, where Machiavelli gave himself wholly to the modes and orders of the "four named above by me." As Machiavelli gives himself to these orders, so an imprudent prince must give himself over to a most prudent man.

The phrase "a most prudent man" was also used only once before, in describing Paulo Vitelli, a mercenary captain. The suggestion is thus planted of a mercenary captain, a "third person," who becomes a "governor" and takes the state. A mercenary captain is one who is professed in the art of war but who has no state. He is the consequence of the division between pope and emperor, hence truly a "third person," who can also be described as the head of a sect. Mercenary arms may be made one's own. The great difficulty that a mercenary captain faces is having enough time to gain authority over the arms given to him, making them into a single body. But it can be done, as shown by the example of Francesco Sforza, who went from being the head of the sects of arms in Italy to becoming duke of Milan. He did so by "proper means and his own great virtue."

Given the lack of prudence brought about by the times, a most virtuous man must become a mercenary captain. If prudence is once again to rule, he must make the arms of others his own and establish his own sect or school of arms. We come to the conclusion that only a prudent prince will understand what to do when counsels are divided. Men always look to their own interests, and they become good only if the prince understands how to impose necessity on them. The prince must follow nature in imposing necessity on human beings, and prudence is the understanding of that necessity.

CHAPTER XXIV

WHY THE PRINCES OF ITALY HAVE LOST THEIR KINGDOM

The chapter begins with a sentence that summarizes the previous section. "The things written above" may refer either to the precepts just given or to all that has been written from the beginning of the work. The remarkable point made is that a new prince can become ancient through prudential observance of what has been written. Writing, or a text, replaces ancient blood. But this also means that a new prince can become a "natural prince," so the distinction between a usurper and a hereditary prince, made in chapter II, disappears.

Prudence and writing are connected to one another. We have seen something of the exercise in prudence that writing may provide. Writing permits the reader to make judgments so that he may, in coming to know Tuscany, easily come to know other provinces. But it is virtuous actions that obligate men, much more so than ancient blood or the customary. Virtuous actions must have an effect, however, in that they must come to be known. They must be performed not for their own sake but in such a way that one gains a reputation for them. Perhaps most important, the good must be enjoyed in the present. That is what virtuous action permits men to do: enjoy the good in the present. Men will forget the past for present benefits, but what of the future? Machiavelli is silent about this point here, but we have seen how men lack foresight and that they do not believe in things of which they have no knowledge from experience.

We are reminded of the remark in chapter X of how a prudent prince can keep the minds of his citizens firm during a siege. Such a prince, we are told now, will not be abandoned if he himself "is not found lacking in other things." It was said then that what was needed were the means of life and of defense. But here the reference is to the person of the prince himself, especially to the "brains" of the prince. The prince must also have those qualities that make him avoid contempt, but we have seen that the qualities are to be used prudently, as the skilled archer uses the virtue of his bow. The brains of the prince or his prudence is what obligates men and provides for his defense.

Machiavelli promises the prince a "double glory," but not a glory here and in the hereafter. The double glory is that of founding and then of ornamenting a principate. The ornaments are good laws, good arms, and good examples. Good laws are, as we know, the result of good arms. The laws are mentioned first, therefore, because they are ornaments. Good examples are the actions taken by the prince. One notices that he does not speak of "rare examples." Perhaps there is also here an implicit contrast with writing. Good writing is not ornamented; it does not display itself. But actions require display if they are to be effective, for how can one be reputed virtuous if one's actions do not bring fame? Actions must be ornamented, as it were, if there is to be glory. Useful writings do not necessarily bring glory. The writer, in fact, conceals himself behind the names that are celebrated.

. . .

We now come to the real topic of the chapter: the question of Italy. We are reminded of the beginning, for the two lords of Italy who are mentioned as having "lost the state in our times" are the king of Naples and the duke of Milan. Milan and Naples can be said to be the two extremes of Italy. The condition of Italy is defined in terms of what has happened to the extremes, but has the state also been lost at the center?

In the title of chapter XXIV *regnum* is in the singular. Therefore, Italy is a single kingdom with many princes in it, and it is these many princes who have lost the kingdom. *Regnum* is used only once before (in chapter VI), in a Latin quotation describing Hiero of Syracuse, which said that all that Hiero needed for ruling was a kingdom.

Curiously, the conquerors of Italy are not mentioned. Machiavelli does not speak directly of Spain or of France as conquerors, although he certainly alludes to them in speaking of Naples and of Milan. The conquerors who are explicitly mentioned are the Romans and the Greeks, but they attacked Philip of Macedon, not Italy. Instead of turning directly to ancient or to modern conquerors of Italy, he is to speak, as he did in chapter III, of the conquest of Greece by the Romans. The Romans did not let Philip's persuasions induce them to be friendly without first putting him down. Philip was one of the principal opponents of the Romans; the other was Antiochus. Apparently the province of Greece suffices as an example, but this time it is an example of how one resists a foreign invader, not how to conquer a foreign province. To whom, then, was the kingdom of Italy lost?

· · ·

The question to ask first is, What is meant by the kingdom of Italy? Is it not strange to refer to Italy as a kingdom? The kingdom of which we have heard the most is the kingdom of Darius, for that is the government whose nature we have been specifically asked to consider. We considered that kingdom again as the kingdom of the Turk; and the Christian pontificate was then said to be similar to the kingdom of the Sultan, that is, the kingdom of the Turk. We thus come to the kingdom at the center of Italy, or the kingdom the Christian pontificate represents, which is said by Machiavelli to have disarmed Italy and delivered her into slavery and contempt. Are we to consider such slavery the occupation or the seizure of Italy?

But what is the kingdom that has been lost? The kingdom that has conquered Italy is the one first mentioned at the beginning of chapter XI; it is the kingdom that is not of this world and therefore neither defends nor governs. What has been lost, then, is the kingdom of this world, the one that must defend and govern and that must have arms, laws, and good examples. To regain the kingdom of Italy is to unite and to arm Italy, but that is necessarily to do away with the papal states or the temporal power of the papacy. But does not Machiavelli mean to go further? What of the hold of the papacy on its soldiers? If that kingdom is to be defeated, must not that hold be broken? More generally, must not regaining the kingdom of Italy include the destruction of the imperium of the papacy, or whatever it is that gives it power over human beings? For as long as that power holds, Italy and all men will be disarmed. One need only be reminded of what has been said of arms in chapter XII.

The two defects that account for the loss of the kingdom by the lords of Italy are the want of arms and the failure to make the people friends, thus securing themselves against the great. States that can put an army into the field are not lost unless they have these defects. Of course, if one can put an army into the field, one surely does not have the defects mentioned. It would seem, then, that the German cities spoken of in chapter X are not examples to be imitated, for they could not put an army into the field.[1] But Machiavelli has also held out hope for those who are besieged and yet have a prince with a firm *animo.*

. . .

We need to consider further the example of Philip of Macedon, the only one given in this chapter. He is not the father of Alexander, and therefore not one of those to whose modes and orders Machiavelli has pledged his faith. Philip, however, was able to put up a protracted resistance to the Romans before he was overcome by Titus Quintius Flamininus, who first appears in *The Prince* (chapter XXI) as an unnamed Roman legate urging the Achaeans not to be neutral. Titus Quintius Flamininus was thirty-three years old when he appeared in Greece. He was a humane man and a lover of philosophy, and it was as a philhellene that he was welcomed as the liberator of Greece. We should remind ourselves, however, that the Romans ended by destroying "many cities in that province in order to hold it."

Philip's resistance to Titus Quintius raises the question of the tactics against such an enemy as the Romans, who are far stronger than one. We recall that Philopoemen also tried to rouse Greek resistance but failed. Philip is given as the example of how one is able to fight a protracted war against a stronger enemy.[2] He may have the dominion over some cities, but he is said to have kept the kingdom.

In order to understand Machiavelli's enigmatic statement, we need to turn to the description of Philip's adventures against the Romans. These adventures are described in several passages in the *Discourses* (II.1, 4; III.10, 37). If we consider these passages, we shall see how subtly Machiavelli has woven his text in chapter XXIV of *The Prince.*

. . .

Regnum was used only once before, in connection with Hiero of Syracuse. Why are we to be reminded of Hiero? In the Dedicatory Letter to the *Discourses,* Hiero is mentioned as one to be preferred to Perseus, the Macedonian, because Hiero is a prince who lacked only a principate. Incidentally, the Philip of Macedon spoken of in chapter XXIV of *The Prince* was the father of that Perseus who was the last king of Macedonia and who, unlike Hiero, inherited a kingdom but lost it.

Discourses is meant to be a private work addressed to Machiavelli's friends, who are said to be like Hiero. They are princes, first men, and one is thus led to wonder whether the phrase "our princes," used in chapter XXIV of *The Prince,* includes such men as Zanobi Buondelmonti and Cosimo Rucellai. Machiavelli has seldom spoken of that which is "ours." Who is included in that possessive pronoun, contemporary Italians in general or the reader with a theoretical interest? Machiavelli does speak of "our matter," addressing himself to the reader who is able to understand (*The Prince* XIX.120). He speaks of what is "ours" in two other places, and in both instances the context is that of the difference between modern princes and ancient ones. He thus speaks of the sins of Italy as "our sins" (*The Prince* XII.72), which are the sins of princes. He also notes the difference between the "princes of our times" and the Roman emperors from Marcus Aurelius to Maximinus (*The Prince* XIX.119). If "our princes" also refers to those who are princes except for a principate, one may also think of the reader whom Machiavelli addresses, or the one for whom he writes: the one who understands.

The beginning of the *Discourses* is addressed to two princes who are so by virtue and not by fortune. In the two prefaces of the *Discourses,* Machiavelli makes it evident that he has taken a way "not yet trodden by anyone" and that he is a discoverer of new modes and orders. In part, he says, his purpose is to teach modern men how to read again, that they may taste the true flavor of the histories. That failure to read is said to be the principal failure of the present age, not either the weaknesses into which the world has been conducted because of "our" religion or the ambitious leisure that prevails in Christian provinces and cities. But in the preface to book II Machiavelli declares that the purpose of his writing is to turn the *animi* of young men from the weakness of present times, making them willing to prepare themselves to imitate ancient times, so that someone may carry his enterprise to completion. His friends are such young men, and they would seem to be the true "princes of our times." If the princes of Italy have lost the kingdom, then these latter princes would seem to be the ones to regain the kingdom. I do not intend to discuss the complexities of the *Discourses* here. Suffice it to note that the *Discourses* is intended for young, would-be princes who, like Hiero, lack only a kingdom to rule.

We return to the question at hand: how is it possible to say that Philip nonetheless kept the kingdom? To answer that question, we need to look at two chapters in the *Discourses.* The first mention we have of Philip of Macedon is in the *Discourses* II.4, a chapter on the three modes of expansion that republics have adopted. The first mode is that observed by the ancient Tuscans, who used a league consisting of several equal republics. Such a mode was also used by the Achaeans and the Aetolians, the very ones who allowed the Romans to come into Greece (*The Prince* III.14). The second mode of conquest is that of the Romans who made companions or allies, placing themselves at the head of the alliance. The third mode is to make subjects and not companions, as did the Spartans and the Athenians. After a long discussion, Machiavelli declares the Roman mode of conquest as the certain and sure one, thus recapitulating the conclusion he had also reached in chapter V of *The Prince.* The Romans, one also recalls, did not listen to the persuasions of Philip but saw to it that he was defeated (*The Prince* III).

Machiavelli returns to the alternative mode of leagues and discusses at length its weaknesses. What Philip of Macedon says is cited as testimony to the truth that leagues offer either protection or their soldiers for money, as the Swiss do "today." Philip accuses the Aetolian league—Philopoemen—of avarice and infidelity, for the league is willing to take service with the enemy, and the ensign of Aetolia can often be seen in two armies opposing each other. Machiavelli concludes that because this mode of leagues is useless to armed republics, it is especially useless to unarmed ones, and thus to the Italian republics. One is to turn not to Tuscany but to Rome, and the crucial testimony, the one that suffices, is that of Philip.

Having come to so clear a conclusion after a lengthy discussion, Machiavelli now proceeds to reverse himself in the last part of *Discourses* II.4. The imitation of the Romans is too difficult; that of the ancient Tuscans is not. The Tuscan's mode permitted them securely to hold power in Italy for a long time and brought them the highest glory of empire and arms, as well as customs and religion worthy of the highest praise. The French and the Romans reduced and then extinguished almost all trace of this power and glory two thousand years ago. To recover the mode of the Tuscans is thus to go back to the most ancient stratum of Italy of which we have any memory—and past the central event of Christian history.

If the Tuscan mode is still to be considered, that of the Spartans and the Athenians is simply to be rejected. To rule others as subjects is most difficult and fatiguing. Sparta and Athens imposed too difficult a rule for a city to follow. The Romans are also difficult to imitate: for some reason, they are the only ones who have used the mode of alliances. What the Romans did was to conquer kings in the provinces outside Italy, and the conquests made the city grow to such exceeding greatness and made it so exceedingly well armed that its allies or companions were helpless against Roman power. The allies conspired against Rome to avenge their injuries, but they were simply crushed, turned into subjects instead of allies.

The peculiar Roman mode, then, is to use the conquest of outside kingdoms to dominate the members of the alliance. The rule of the Romans was accepted because it appeared at first as if the member republics were to be left to rule themselves with their own laws in a league of equals, but that was only the appearance. The truth was the domination of one city, Rome. That domination would not have been possible, however, without the conquest of outside provinces.

We have seen that the Romans did subjugate provinces that previously enjoyed liberty, such as Spain, France, and Greece. We are thus reminded not only of the conquest of the republics of Italy but also of the free provinces of the world. Indeed, we are led to the conclusion that the loss of liberty in Italy and elsewhere was caused by the Romans.

If one wishes, then, to preserve Italian liberty, it would seem that one could not follow Roman modes. The more liberty becomes important, the more the Tuscan mode is the only alternative left. It is, at the same time, the easiest one to imitate.

We may now appreciate the Machiavellian jest if we think of the choices placed before "our" Italian princes. First, they may join the Tuscan league, which has shown that it can provide power and glory, where the princes will be equals; second, they may choose to be made companions or allies of a city that pretends to be a league of equals but that turns out to be the domination of a single city, using the power derived from outside kingdoms and provinces to destroy liberty within; or, third, they simply put themselves under the rule of a single city, as was the policy of Sparta and Athens—which we interpret to be the rule of the best regime.

We must now reconsider the testimony given by Philip when he was in amicable conference with Titus Quintius. The bad faith attributed to the Aetolians and to leagues generally is balanced by the subsequent statement that leagues can bring great glory. Is Philip to be taken as approving of either the Roman mode or that of the Spartans?

Before we make any final judgment of Philip, we should turn to III.10 of the *Discourses,* where he is cited as a special example out of a thousand. He is an example of how a captain cannot avoid a battle when the adversary wishes to have battle "in every mode." The topic, in other words, is the present one, of how Philip sustained himself in the war against the Romans.

When he was attacked by the Romans, Philip decided not to join battle. He went instead to the summit of a mountain and fortified it, judging that the Romans would not dare go to find him. They did, however, and chased him from that mountain. Not being able to resist, he fled with most of his people. What saved him from being wholly consumed was the iniquity of the country, which prevented the Romans from following him. He came to know, then, by experience, that it was not enough to stand on a mountain. However, not wishing to be enclosed in towns (*terre*), he deliberated and decided to take another mode, which was to stay many miles distant from the Roman camp. But he soon saw that by prolonging the war in this way the condition of his army was worsening and his subjects were being oppressed by the enemy. He therefore determined to try his fortune in battle. Machiavelli is silent on the outcome of the battle, in which Philip was defeated at Cynoscephalae (A.D. 197) by Titus Quintius Flamininus.

We see that Philip does not wish to take the expedient of sustaining a long siege. Is that an error? We have been assured, after all, that a prudent prince can withstand a long siege. Having been alerted by this time to the Machiavellian mode of suggesting clues, we wonder whether the error stems from an unwillingness to accept the earth as the only place the human being has.

This account of Philip in the *Discourses* has been described as "the further adventures" of an opponent of Christianity.[3] What that captain learns by experience is that he cannot stay on the summit, or high above everyone; he must descend to the valleys, where human life goes on. But in not wishing to be limited to the human sphere, the only expedient left to Philip is distance. Not only is distance a question of space, however, it can also be a question of time. Machiavelli declares that a captain who does not wish to fight has no remedy other than to put himself at a distance of at least fifty miles (years?) from the enemy. How is it possible for the captain to place himself at some distance in time? The answer would seem to be found in the capacity of the writer to overcome time. A writer-captain, such as Machiavelli, can speak to one more beloved of Heaven whenever fortune gives the occasion.

. . .

In the beginning of the *Discourses* we are told explicitly that Philip cannot be the captain to serve as the exemplar of how one preserves the kingdom against a more powerful enemy. How, then, can Machiavelli say in *The Prince* that Philip nonetheless kept the kingdom?

We may paraphrase the argument as follows. The Romans conquered Greece and extinguished its liberty, and Philip was unable finally to defend Greece. His modes, then, ought not be imitated by those who wish to recover liberty. Nonetheless, his adventures show, by experience, the alternatives that may be taken by those who would learn from that great defeat. We are to learn from the Romans how one may conquer, even if in the end we are to use not Roman modes but Tuscan ones.[4] This Philip was not able to do what a former Philip and his successor did. But this much lesser ancient captain—one who remains lesser even when taken in proportion—nevertheless retained the kingdom, at least in part. In other words, the conquest of Greece was not as final as everyone has perhaps thought. The "iniquity of the country" saved Philip; that is, the iniquity of nature, both human and otherwise, saved him from being "wholly consumed." Perhaps, then, the kingdom can never be wholly lost. And there are many modes that a prudent prince may use first to defend and then to attack—perhaps a fortified town, perhaps distance, perhaps a league. What is certain is that one can no longer go the way of Sparta or Athens.

. . .

Machiavelli ends the chapter by calling on "our princes" to accuse not fortune but their indolence. We have been assured that, despite the greatness of the conqueror, one can prepare good, certain, and durable defenses. But can one do this in the midst of the tempest (and are we in its midst?), or is it still possible quietly to prepare the defenses that can easily turn into modes of offense? One must not wait if one is to have proper defenses; one ought to think of more than flight. (Philip of Macedon was said to have incurred dishonor for running away.) Machiavelli seems to suggest that one can lose and yet acquire glory. Thus the challenge to the Romans is to be made; battle is not to be avoided.

The challenge must be made because one cannot depend on the people to tire of the insolence of the conqueror. The people can do nothing by themselves. Have the philosophers especially thought of being rescued by the people? One suspects that this is Machiavelli's comment on the Socratic dictum that the wise man does not seek rule but waits for the people to come to him (*Republic* 489b–c). The comment can now be read as pungent and to the point: "Such a remedy, when others are lacking, is good, but it is very bad indeed to have let go other remedies for this one, for one should never fall believing that someone will be found to pick you up." Such a course is ignoble. That is the greatest accusation made against the classical political philosophers. Machiavelli's prince will not wait but will offer battle in every mode.

The last sentence calls on the would-be prince to depend on "you yourself and on your virtue." We are reminded that, according to Machiavelli, David did not depend on anyone else.

NOTES

1. Indeed, to be caught in a town (*terra*) is what should be avoided, as Philip of Macedon did when he waged war against the Romans and Greece (*Discourses* III.10).

2. One can read of the strategy and tactics of Philip of Macedon in the *Discourses*. Although I have tried to avoid referring to the *Discourses* as a means of explicating *The Prince,* it does seem to me that we are invited to look at the way in

which he resisted the Romans. It is especially with respect to Philip that one sees how condensed and allusive *The Prince* actually is.

3. See Harvey C. Mansfield, *Machiavelli's New Modes and Orders: A Study of the Discourses on Livy* (Ithaca, N.Y.: Cornell University Press, 1979), 352.

4. See chapters XIV and XV of this book.

CHAPTER XXV

HOW MUCH FORTUNE IS ABLE TO DO IN HUMAN THINGS AND IN WHAT MODE ONE MAY OPPOSE HER

Machiavelli begins by replying to an objection to the possibility of a good, certain, and durable defense against fortune. His reply is also addressed to those who think that men can do nothing but wait for fortune to provide an occasion. Many have held and still hold the opinion that human prudence is helpless before fortune and God alike, or before either fortune or God. Are fortune and God to be distinguished, or are they the same? Such a judgment about the helplessness of prudence would seem to be the practical consequence of the opinion that the wise man should not seize rule but rather should wait for the people to come to him. To believe in fortune and God would seem to be the same as to believe that the people will pick one up when one falls. It is to depend on matter, and therefore on chance, for one then waits for the chance combinations of matter to provide the occasion. And to wait for the occasion is to believe in fortune. This belief is especially dominant in "our times," and we are reminded of what was said in chapter XII about the condition of Italy.

We see that to be governed by chance is the same as to be governed by fortune or God. To be so dependent is ignoble, for one is then "without remedy" for human ills. "Our" times are given over to chance, and that has led to changes beyond any human conjecture, to miracles. Machiavelli declares himself inclined in part to this opinion. But how far he does agree, or precisely to what part he inclines, is unclear. He may agree, for example, that lack of prudence has permitted chance to have greater influence; thus Italian losses can be miraculous. To the rule of chance we may oppose human "sweat," that is, human industry, work, and care. "To sweat" is to believe that men can correct things, that human prudence is not helpless, and that man is not given over to the rule of matter. Such a belief would require disbelief in the rule of fortune and God, which is simply the rule of chance.

Machiavelli puts forward a new belief, which he first calls a judgment, that would not wholly contradict the belief in fortune. He judges that fortune rules half of human actions. Why he gives half to fortune is explained by the changes he has seen in "our times," which confirms the opinion of "many." Is the equal division of jurisdictions between prudence and fortune simply arbitrary? We are tempted to ask whether human beings are subject to fortune insofar as they are beastly, given that Machiavelli divides human nature into halves. However that may be, the half of human actions given to fortune seems to be that of unquiet or adverse times. When fortune becomes angry, it is like violent rivers—one notes the change from the singular to the plural. Is human life to be thought of as equally divided between quiet and troubled times, or between peace and war? In quiet times men can prepare defenses or use their prudence so that they are not overwhelmed and destroyed in unquiet times. As rivers can be contained within embankments, so fortune's anger may also be contained. Instead, then, of giving fortune any jurisdiction over human actions, Machiavelli has wholly taken away her power. Fortune demonstrates her power only if there is no ordered virtue to resist her.

Ordered virtue seems to be the orders to which Machiavelli gave himself, the orders that give men arms to defend themselves. Ordered virtue is good laws, good arms, and good examples. We now see that the defenses of which he previously spoke are meant to defend and to attack not only dangers that arise from human actions but also chance itself, or the motions of matter.

Only a proper political order can defend against rivers and therefore against fortune. Rivers may destroy trees and buildings and may change the land itself, but are they full of malice and ill will toward human beings? Or are they uncaring about human ends? Natural forces are not directed to human ends; Machiavelli denies that there is a teleology in things. If they are not directed to human ends, can they be, and is that, in fact, what ordered virtue does? Only ordered virtue can direct the natural motions of things to human ends, and that becomes the political task.

Virtue must be given a definite order or shape by the political founder, and that alone can save human beings. The task of political order is to defend human beings from the destructiveness of chance, fortune, or God, none of which cares for man or his works. The discovery of man's defenselessness in an uncaring universe seems to be the spur that incites men to exercise prudence. The belief in the power of human prudence requires disbelief in powers or a power that cares for human beings.

Machiavelli, however, began not with a providential world but with one that was ruled by fortune. The difficulty was human quietism, the failure of men to do anything about their condition. The ambiguity arises from the fact that a belief in providence or God would end in a similar quietism. Thus Machiavelli conflates the beliefs in fortune and in God into a belief in the rule of chance. He then indicates that the rule of chance is to be understood as giving rise to a belief in the possibility of miracles. If the rule of chance and the rule of providence are the same—and there is no doubt that Machiavelli makes that identification—then disbelief in providence would be the first step to a restoration of human prudence. Machiavelli is clearly convinced that the most drastic steps are necessary to bring about the possibility of what he calls "ordered virtue."

. . .

The reader is now to consider Italy. In chapter XXIV the reader was not directly addressed; instead, the princes were addressed in the third person plural. Here, however, the addressee is once again the reader with a theoretical interest.

Italy is without ordered virtue, without defenses; hence it is subject to a flood that has brought about great changes in our time. The flood and these changes need not have come. How is Italy the seat of these changes and the one that put them into motion? We recall that the flood of the French invasion was immediately caused by the church, but the truer cause is that Italy is disarmed. Italy disarmed is mankind disarmed, for what is at issue is ultimately the contention between the City of God and the City of Man. If Machiavelli is right, then to liberate Italy is to liberate mankind.

Machiavelli has now said everything he wishes to say generally about opposing fortune. It can be summarized as follows: Explicitly, he has said that fortune is the arbiter of half of our actions; that she is like a violent river or a natural force that turns against human beings, but that she can be defended against; and that of all countries Italy is especially subject to fortune, because she is undefended. We are also led to understand that chance, God, and fortune do not simply rule the world; that natural forces are not directed to human ends and that whatever is specifically human must be made by man himself; that, therefore, the only instrument man has of defending himself against nature and God, or chance and fortune, is ordered virtue or human prudence; and that man is without defense if he remains under the illusion of providence or that he is cared for, that nature is ordered toward human ends. This first part of chapter XXV makes clear that belief in God is the cause of man's lack of defenses.

. . .

The turn to particulars is a discussion of how each individual prince governs the things of the world. Machiavelli is to explain why a prince succeeds and then fails without changing his nature or any of his qualities. He says, "I believe," twice. He has not spoken of what he believes since he said that he believed in cruelty well used. He did speak of what he did not believe twice in chapter XX, when he discussed factions. He did not believe that to use factions was a wise precept for "our times." He is, therefore, not making a judgment, that is, making a considered response, stating an opinion, or coming to a conclusion. He is exact in his language: a belief has a different status from a conclusion that is the result of a chain of reasoning. Indeed, the difficulty or, perhaps, impossibility of coming to a reasoned conclusion is what makes one have to state a proposition as a belief.

What Machiavelli believes is that the prince is happy when his "modes" are at one with the times. "Modes" are the natural inclinations of each man to proceed in a certain way—whether, for example, he proceeds cautiously or recklessly. Modes are particular or individual; they seem to be associated with the "matter" or the bodily character of a prince, much as a country has a natural disposition to republican rule or to princely rule.

The only ends men have in view are glory and riches. The end of human actions is not virtue, since the natural and ordinary desire of human beings is to acquire. Machiavelli has suggested that human beings are always in need, but nowhere in *The Prince* does he make that point explicit. We must make the connection between the two statements. Men must acquire if they are to preserve themselves; this may be especially true of princes, but it is true of all human beings. They cannot be concerned with virtue because they cannot do so; all their thought, all their industry, must be turned to making capital in quiet times in order to be able to defend themselves in adversity. In recent times, men have lived under illusions: they have forgotten the harshness of necessity. Thus the acquisition of glory and riches is the only effectual end men have, and Machiavelli now states it openly for the first time in his own name.

We also see that the good changes. The difficulty is that men do not change as circumstances change. No man is so prudent that he can act against his natural inclinations, and he thus fails because he fails to change his nature. The conclusion thus seems to be that the prince depends on the times or on fortune. Because men cannot go against their natures, they are prisoners of nature or of fortune. Fortune, or chance, is what gives man his nature and, of greater import, brings it about that his nature and the times are in concord. If they are not, he suffers from the malignity of fortune; and that may even be a "great and continuous malignity."

We have seen, however, that it is necessary for a prince to be good and not good, using each according to necessity. The good varies—or, rather, seems to vary—because a prudent man must depart from what is held to be good and move toward that which will save the state. We are now told that, on the contrary, it is almost impossible for men to change their natures, that is, to change from one quality to another. Such an alternation is to go against one's nature, and no man is so prudent that he can do this; yet it is what a prince needs to do. Machiavelli has simply restated, in an even stronger way, the power of fortune and the weakness of prudence.

In the pairs of modes listed, violence and art are apparently to be understood as contrary to one another. Yet Severus, the example of the contrasting natures of the fox and the lion, proceeded, as these natures imply, with both art and violence. Indeed, the very definition of prudence is the capacity to alternate between the human and the beastly and, of the beastly, between the fox and the lion. The only conclusion to which one can come is that Machiavelli's account is here, once again, misleading, which should by this time be not at all surprising.

What is said about the difficulty of changing one's modes is truer of peoples than of princes. Peoples have natural inclinations that persist and are changed only with the utmost difficulty. We also need to recall that the people are brought to believe in a prince's orders and modes and that he cannot therefore appear to change even when change is required. Thus the natural prince was said to have an advantage, in that changes could be made insensibly. And, of course, a prince needs to learn how to deceive, to manipulate appearances so that he may never seem to go against pity, faith, humanity, integrity, or religion. Thus it is the people who cannot depart from their modes, forcing the prince especially to use the fox. Such a prince would then always appear never to change, and that would be the opinion no one would dare to challenge. If each prince attains the ends he has before him, then everyone will regard his actions as never having deviated from what people have taken him to be. Success, in other words, ensures that he will be regarded as an "ancient prince," and his reputation will be that he has all the qualities that are regarded as good.

. . .

The only example given in the chapter of men's different modes of proceeding, and of whether they succeed, is that of Pope Julius II. The pope proceeded impetuously and succeeded in all that he did. The chapter ends with the conclusion that it is better to be impetuous than cautious, because fortune varies and men remain obstinately with their modes. The example to be followed is, therefore, that of Julius, whose motion left others suspended in amazement. Impetuosity thus signifies that one remains in motion, beyond all human prudence.

Impetuous motion is therefore not prudence. Instead, it is the substitute for prudence. The argument is that men cannot or will not be prudent; because they cannot change their modes, they should adopt one mode: to be impetuous.

Machiavelli's praise of Julius is qualified by the remark that only his brief life saved him. Despite the acknowledgment that failure would necessarily have come, Machiavelli nonetheless goes on to praise his mode, ending with the notorious advice that one should beat and knock down fortune, for fortune is a woman and enjoys such displays of mastery. Such advice, to use Machiavelli's language, seems to go against all human prudence.

If we keep in mind that what is said of Julius is that he indeed proceeds beyond any human prudence, one begins to wonder about how we are to judge his actions. Does Julius proceed with a suprahuman prudence or a prudence that claims to be suprahuman? One also wonders which Julius is meant: one can think of another Julius who was also a pontiff, who also proceeded beyond all human prudence and with similar results, and who perhaps also escaped having to change his mode because of the brevity of his rule.

However that may be, we see that instead of trying to change one's nature to fit the times and circumstances, one simply goes straight to whatever one desires and seizes it. One need not exercise art, calculation, caution, and patience; ferocity and motion are the qualities to be adopted. The advice to be impetuous, however, works only if men cannot be prudent. We have seen that the result of a belief in the weakness of prudence is laziness or the opinion that it does not do "to sweat much over things." The belief in impetuous motion replaces the belief in quiet rest, but both proceed from the same understanding of the weakness of human prudence.

That fortune may be conquered by impetuous motion is a belief, to be given the same regard as the belief that one cannot do anything about fortune. The greater the possibility that men can act prudently, the less credence we give to either opinion. Does Machiavelli replace the indolence that arises from a belief in providence with the impetuosity that can arise from a belief in fortune? In either case, the belief that underlies both of these is in a personal being who acts either to favor or to oppose the designs of men. In other words, the Machiavellian enterprise against the biblical God is concealed in the description of how the goddess Fortuna may be conquered. The imitation of Fortuna suggested in chapter XX becomes her rape in chapter XXV.

The new story that is to be told—the one that is to govern the new world Machiavelli is opening up—is the story of the omnicompetence of human beings to deal with the things of the world. The mode or temper is immediate and quick action, in the fundamental belief that all obstacles can be overcome and that the audacity of youth is better than the caution of age. Such a mode cannot be called prudent, but most human beings are not, after all, capable of prudence.

Machiavelli prefers this mode because it is the mode that destroys the hold of the customary and thus brings forth a character that is without any respect, one that will bring about disbelief in a providential world. Impetuous motion may not be prudence, but it removes a thousand excuses and a thousand fears. Whether impetuousness is a better temperament than prudence to govern the world is still being debated—and will, no doubt, continue to be.

. . .

To act virtuously appears to be, in Machiavelli's understanding, to act according to necessity. Prudence is knowing from afar what needs to be done. To be more exact, to have virtue is to have those qualities that enable one to enter into and to escape from dangers, to stand up to and to overcome adverse things. That may require changing from one quality to another. The ability to change from one quality to another, as the nature of things demands, is prudence. One may have greatness of mind and high intentions, ferocity, and virtue, as did Cesare Borgia, yet have little prudence. Prudence is what establishes a prince, makes him secure, obligates men to him, and introduces his form into the given matter. How a prince appears to other men and whether he gains the fame of being a great man and one of excellent mind depend on his qualities or virtues—and these are judged by the eyes. Only prudence, however, will enable him to pick the right mode, or the one least inconvenient or bad, that the times demand.

. . .

The necessity that princes must confront is that of acquisition, of gaining the end that each human being wants: glory and riches. Riches one easily understands, for men always wish to prosper and have much. But one gains glory by beginning a new principate or by establishing a new order. If one is a prince one has, of course, the riches of a people at one's command. One also, however, needs to give the people the order that enables them to enjoy the benefits of the time. One cannot have glory, in other words, unless one establishes the ordered virtue that defends human beings against the variations of chance.

Necessity may further be explained as the neediness in which all men find themselves. If the motions of nature are not directed to human ends, the greatest need is the mastery of these motions, either such that they are directed to human ends or such that human beings are protected from the changes they undergo.

The further necessity with which the prince must be concerned is that one cannot rely on the people. They do not and cannot understand what is truly necessary. They are taken by the appearances of things and by what is immediately beneficial; they prefer that to which they are accustomed, and they act generally under one illusion or another, especially under the illusion that man is beloved by the gods or is the cared-for darling of the cosmos. Thus the prince must be concerned with appearances, with reputation, and with what is effective with the many. He must make this choice because there is no other way to provide human beings with what they need. The love of glory and riches is unquestionably vulgar, but the world has no place for anything but the vulgar. The prince ends by thinking more of others than of himself; he descends from the high places where he would perhaps prefer to be because he recognizes that his concern must be the illusions men have, not his understanding of the nature of things. He must be concerned with glory and riches because he is philanthropic, because he cares more about others than he cares about himself. If human beings are to be defended and their liberty regained, the princes of this world must be persuaded to turn to what all men desire.

CHAPTER XXVI

EXHORTATION TO LAY HOLD OF ITALY AND VINDICATE HER LIBERTY FROM THE BARBARIANS

To vindicate Italy's liberty from the barbarians is, in the first place, to lay claim to it, and in so doing to deliver and protect it. It also means to take vengeance and to punish those who have presumed to arrogate what rightfully belongs to one. Having reflected on the condition of Italy and the cause of the loss of the kingdom, and having seen that the dominance of fortune in human affairs has its seat in Italy, we now are told that Italy is yearning—indeed, trembling—with expectation to see her redeemer. The language reminds one of the biblical expectation of the Messiah in the fullness of time, or of a woman expecting her lover. The matter of Italy is wholly disposed to receive its form, awaiting the one who will introduce that which will give honor to him and good to the *università* of human beings who are of that matter—or are of the general body of that matter.

Italy is matter yearning for form, but we are not explicitly told whether it is naturally predisposed to one single form. That a specific form for Italy may exist, however, is suggested by the references to an Italian spirit and to Italian virtue. It has also been said that a proper occasion is needed if the form of a founder is to be introduced. The coincidence of form and matter seems to come about by chance. That occasion is now present for one who would be a founder. We have returned to the most excellent, celebrated men of chapter VI, who seem to depend on fortune and proceed by imitation. Notably, one name, that of Romulus, has been omitted. In a discussion of the liberation of Italy and a restoration of ancient Italian virtue, that omission is as strange as would be the omission of Moses' name in a discussion of a restoration of the Covenant of Sinai for Israel.

We are immediately brought to the possibility that God may have ordained a certain man to redeem Italy. Fortune, however, has rejected him. God has therefore turned against him, for we know that God and fortune are said to rule the things of the world. If one depends on there being an occasion for one's virtue—as are all the founders named, with the exception of Romulus—one is shown to be vulnerable to the whims of God, or fortune, or chance. One is, in other words, like the princes who depend on the fortune and the arms of another.

Italy prays to God to be redeemed, and the House of the Medici is said to be favored by God and the church. We have heard before of the greatness that fortune promises Lorenzo. Lorenzo is certainly not a Moses or a Cyrus, or even a Hiero; instead, he is entirely dependent on the fortune of another.

The man who has been reprobated by fortune is usually said to be Cesare Borgia. However, could not the reference be to Machiavelli himself? He too has suffered from fortune, and, unlike anyone else mentioned in *The Prince,* he has suffered from a continuous malignity of fortune. We are reminded, however, that Machiavelli is not like the men who are called most excellent; he is more like Xenophon. The status of Machiavelli is revealed, as we have seen, most clearly in chapter XV, where he is not an imitator but has departed from the ways of others, striking out on a new path. How subject is he to fortune, especially when he has said that the written things, observed prudently, enable one to establish a new order? In this context, the new order is the introduction of a new form into Italy, and that in turn reminds one of the need to regain the kingdom of Italy.

The paragraph that follows is perhaps the most puzzling in the entire work. The redemption of Italy is said not to be very difficult, especially if one recalls "the actions and the lives of those named above." To recall such actions is to be reminded of the thousand hardships and dangers facing the founder: how he must make many spirited and dangerous decisions, stand up to adversities, be without faith, pity, and religion, and be ready to be as brutal and deceptive as Severus.

Instead of the self-sufficient founder who stands on his own and does not beg, the Medici are told that God is a friend who will make things easy for them. The easiness of the task is to be made manifest by "extraordinary things"—here *extraordinary* has the meaning of *miraculous.* Is this reassurance intended to persuade the Medici to be as impetuous as Julius in their actions?

The extraordinary things mentioned are the signs given to Moses and the people of Israel in their journey to the Promised Land, but Machiavelli rearranges the sequence of signs; that is, he gives them a new order. God, however, does not want to do everything Himself, and we are reminded that only half of our actions are to be attributed to fortune. Once again, it would appear that God and fortune are interchangeable.

What does Machiavelli mean when he says that such extraordinary things have occurred in Italy? The only extraordinary things that have occurred are the seven battles that are subsequently mentioned and that have also been called "sudden and miraculous losses." These are the examples that had led Machiavelli to discuss the origins and progress of mercenary arms in Italy "from on high." However, the "extraordinary things" are not said to have occurred in Italy; what Machiavelli does say is that "here" are to be seen such things. "Here" could mean the text itself. After all, these signs are also spoken of in a Book, just as they are here now spoken of in another book. And if Moses had a Book, so Lorenzo has one; and if that one gave signs, so does this one.

Furthermore, extraordinary things seem to occur for all who would found new orders. Cyrus speaks to God as much as Moses does, and God is equally a friend to all men who are rare and marvelous. God conducts extraordinary things for these men—or, rather, is it Xenophon and his kind who make extraordinary things happen? For is Cyrus not a character in Xenophon's book?

One other conclusion must be drawn. If one depends on the extraordinary, one depends on chance, not prudence. The Medici depend on fortune and the extraordinary. Machiavelli speaks of their fortune and virtue only; he does not mention their prudence. And we recall that in the Epistle Dedicatory he did not even speak of Lorenzo's virtues, only of his qualities. What virtues the Medici have would seem to be possessed by Pope Leo X, whose "goodness and infinite other virtues" will, Machiavelli hopes, make that pontificate great and venerated—yet Machiavelli is silent throughout about their prudence.

Moreover, Machiavelli seems to contrast the "one" who is reprobated by fortune with the Medici. The Medici clearly do not have "one" who can take up the banner, one who is so superior that others will yield to him. Such a one must have virtue and fortune, but he must also be a discoverer of new laws and new orders. Machiavelli lays claim to being such a discoverer; indeed, he is the only one who dares to make such a claim. He does not, however, have the fortune and the virtue of House of the Medici. Machiavelli declares that "it is nothing to marvel at if not one of the Italians" has been able to take up the banner of redemption. Yet how can one hope that the Medici can do what "one" is supposed to do? Even if they have fortune and virtue, they certainly are not discoverers of new laws that would make them revered and wonderful. Does someone like Machiavelli need to use those who are like the Medici? As the unarmed prophets, or the writers, conceal themselves behind the most excellent men, so Machiavelli conceals himself behind the ambitions of the Medici who are to follow the example of those excellent men who have redeemed their provinces. Or does Machiavelli suggest a way whereby he who has discovered new modes and orders can make himself so superior that others will indeed yield to him? Will the signs that appear here suffice to make the way easy?

All of the Italians Machiavelli has named have failed, but that is nothing at which to marvel. Is the reference here to Lombardy, Tuscany, and Naples, or is it to all the Italian captains he has previously named? However that may be, Italian military virtue seems to be extinguished because her ancient orders have not been good. Have all the ancient orders, then, been bad? Would not such a general statement necessarily include Roman and Tuscan orders? To discover new orders must be understood to be a rejection of all previous Italian orders, for otherwise would they be new?

If the Italians have previously failed because of defects in their ancient orders, Italian virtue continues to exist, but only in the members, that is, in individuals. The question is not so much a lack of knowing as it is a failure of those who know to be able to take command. Everyone seems to know what to do, but the ones who do know are not obeyed. To be obeyed requires fortune and virtue, and these are the attributes the Medici have.

The failure of Italy in the war against the French is the failure to keep the barbarian or foreign power from becoming dominant. All the ancient orders have proved to be defective in this war against the foreign power. The few who have known what to do cannot command obedience. The only indication we have as to how the few who know might enforce obedience is in the appeal to the Medici. The difficulty of being obeyed is manifested by the need to exhort the Medici. Machiavelli clearly says that it is he who knows the orders to be followed: the way is easy for the liberator of Italy, provided that whoever takes up the banner "takes as a target those orders I have proposed." Machiavelli needs, however, a magnificent one—one who has been made a prince by fortune—to take up the orders he proposes.

The true foundation of the enterprise is the ordering of one's own arms. Machiavelli's enterprise ultimately depends, then, on his providing his own arms. How he is to do this is not discussed here; it is, however, the subject of the *Discourses*. An order must be given to Italian virtue, so that what now exists only in individuals may exist in a single body. Only with such an order can there be a defense against external powers. Stated otherwise, the knowledge that existed here and there in a few "heads" must be turned into an enterprise, an organized body commanded by a prince. The promise the prince gives to these former heads is that they will be honored and "entertained"; that is, they will be provided for in every way.[1]

. . .

The proposed new order may be based on Italian virtue or on Italian matter, but it will be a departure from all Italian orders. It will be a "third order," neither Swiss nor Spanish, that is, neither ancient nor modern. The Swiss and German orders are said to be the same, and we see that German orders follow ancient ones. The Spanish are ruled by the "first king of the Christians," and their orders are therefore, in Machiavelli's own terms, not ancient but modern. The Spanish infantry cannot stand up to horses; in other words, they are vulnerable to the arms especially con-

nected with aristocracy, or the arms of the few. Specifically, this infantry cannot defend itself against the French cavalry. Apparently, the praise of infantry given in
chapter XII must be qualified. French arms, which are mixed, have come to depend
on Swiss infantry. Spanish infantry, however, is superior to Swiss infantry, or to ancient infantry, because of its greater flexibility. German infantry is one that depends
on fortresses or, perhaps, may be said to be fortresslike in its lack of flexibility.
Thus a "Christian infantry," the Spanish or a Christian order that is based on the
people, exists.

Ancient infantry cannot stand up to modern infantry, but modern infantry is unable to withstand cavalry. What is needed is a new form of infantry. A new order of
arms always implies a new order of laws. Arms cannot be divided from the whole
of a people's modes and orders. To change the order of arms is to change the whole
of one's orders; that is to say, it is a change of regimes or constitutions. What is being proposed is an entirely new way of life for human beings, a new understanding
of both God and man, of nature and political order. We have, of course, been speaking of that new understanding throughout.

. . .

The final paragraph of *The Prince* is indeed a passionate exhortation to take the
occasion and to liberate Italy. The call is to let Italy see "the one" who is her redeemer. Machiavelli never says that the redeemer is of the House of the Medici;
what he does say is that if the House of the Medici takes up the task of liberating
Italy, it can do so with that spirit and hope with which all just enterprises are taken
up. The redeemer is the one who will be met with love, faith, and piety. No peoples
will deny him obedience, no envy oppose him, no Italian deny him homage. Machiavelli contradicts what he has previously told us of why no Italian has been able to
restore military virtue. Instead, he assures us that everyone has become disgusted
with the rule of the barbarians. Perhaps only when everyone is disgusted with barbarian rule will the redeemer be welcomed.

Machiavelli calls on the Medici to "nobilitate" or to ennoble "this fatherland"
under their banner. The reference is once again sufficiently ambiguous to make one
wonder which fatherland is meant. Moreover, what is the relationship between the
redeemer called for and the House of the Medici? They do not seem to be one and
the same. Cannot this fatherland be ennobled under the banner of the redeemer
himself? Why must he use the banner and the auspices of another house? Must the
redeemer conceal himself in the house of another?

The Petrarchean *canzone* quoted by Machiavelli was written as an appeal "to the
leaders of Italy" to unite against "the German fury." The call is to virtue and valor,
yet it is not virtue and valor but knowledge that will finally rescue Italy. Machiavelli
is clear on this point. Knowledge, however, is not that which makes others cede,
that is, willing to obey.

In the *Florentine Histories* another Petrarchean *canzone* is said to have moved
Stefano Porcari to attempt a conspiracy "to see if he could take his fatherland out of

the hands of prelates and return her to the ancient life, since he hoped by this, when it would succeed, to be called a new founder and second father of the city." Machiavelli then comments:

> It was known to Messere Stefano that poets many times are full of the divine and prophetic spirit, so that he judged that in every mode those things which Petrarch had prophesied in the *canzone* would come to pass, and that he would be the one who would be the executor of so glorious an enterprise—since it seemed to him that by eloquence, by doctrine, by grace and by friends that he was superior to every other Roman.[2]

Poets are prophets, but are they armed or unarmed? What the poet calls for is the liberation of the fatherland, and perhaps that is the true task of all those who write. Is Machiavelli now using the mouth of Petrarch, as Virgil used Dido? Does Machiavelli believe that the battle will be short, or are we to be as skeptical of Petrarch as we are of the "extraordinary things without example" that were previously mentioned? Stefano Porcari's conspiracy was discovered by the pontiff, and his plot failed. Thirst for vengeance, obstinate faith, piety, tears, obedience, homage, spirit, hope, and, in the case of Porcari, appetite for glory seem to come to nothing, to be ineffective in the final event, for knowledge and prudence are what establish the ordered virtue that defends men.

NOTES

1. One may reflect on what has happened to those who bear the title of *philosophiae doctor* and ask whether they have been ordered into one body and honored and "entertained."

2. *Florentine Histories,* translated by Laura F. Banfield and Harvey C. Mansfield Jr. (Princeton, N.J.: Princeton University Press, 1988), VI.29: 263.

CONCLUSION:
ON THE ORDER OF THE ARGUMENT IN *THE PRINCE*

We may now reconsider the order of the argument in *The Prince*. In chapter XIV, Machiavelli divides the training of the prince into two parts, that of the body and that of the intellect. That preparation is what enables the prince to discuss with his friends how to attack an enemy; it enables the prince to wage war. Writing provides both kinds of exercise. It is the hunt, the learning of the countryside by experience, the exercise of the body. It is also the imitation of great men and their actions, the exercise of the intellect.

The other principle of ordering in the work is suggested in the exhortation to liberate Italy. The Epistle Dedicatory and chapter XXVI frame the argument within the appeal to the Medici, or those favored by fortune and virtue, to take up the banner of liberation. The enterprise of Italy, or the liberation of Italy, is the most evident structuring principle, for the two ordering principles are united by the fact that the enterprise of Italy is the hunt. The question is, What is the meaning of the liberation of Italy?

. . .

Chapters I through V are the beginning of the hunt, with the hunt understood as learning how to wage war by learning how to conquer a foreign province. The foreign province, oddly enough, is Italy. We are to learn how to hunt by coming to know the hillocks, valleys, rivers, and marshes of Tuscany, or the high places and low places. What is especially to be discussed, as we saw in chapter XIV, is how to take a certain hill or a certain high place. Who dwells on that high place? Only, of course, some kind of prince, for it is princes who dwell on high.

Chapter I is a general introduction to the discussion of principates, with the notable absence of any mention of the ecclesiastical principate. Chapter II takes up the question of what a natural prince is. We are still, in other words, in the introductory chapters of *The Prince*. Machiavelli has now identified the object of the hunt and the hunter: the object is how to govern and to maintain the principate; the hunter is the one who is the natural prince, the one who is "naturally" first among men. The question is, What is a natural prince? That question is not answered until chapter XXIV.

Chapter III is the beginning of the hunt proper, the invasion of Italy by France. The *Mandragola* also begins with a crossing of the Alps, and there the hunt is for the most beautiful and chaste woman in Florence. Chapter IV opens up the possibility of universal acquisition. Is there not another suggestion as to what the hunt is, in the reference to Alexander and his successors? Why does Machiavelli choose Alexander and not Caesar? One reason may be that Alexander is the one who conquered Asia, or the kingdom of Darius, or the kingdom of the Turk.

Chapter V speaks of the difficulty of extirpating ancient modes and orders, or the difficulty of destroying the free life. The hatred and desire for vengeance remains, no matter how much time has passed, "for the memory of ancient liberty does not leave them, nor can it let them rest." It is a reassurance for those who love liberty and those under the rule of the Romans, which one may also interpret in terms of another Rome.

. . .

In chapters VI through XI the ally and the enemy of the enterprise of Italy are identified. We turn from the hunt to the beginning of the war itself. Chapter VI indicates that Cyrus is the one great founder to be discussed. The reader is especially to consider the kingdom of Cyrus, the kingdom that claims universal dominion over mankind. As is usual in Machiavelli, the example of Cyrus has two sides to it. On the one hand, one must learn from Cyrus, not Moses, about how one becomes a prince; on the other hand, Cyrus is also the enemy of liberty, as the Turk is the enemy of the Greek and of the free life.

Chapter VII is about the conquest from within, especially about acquisition without fortune and arms or even an occasion. Chapter VII indicates that he who would conquer Italy need not wait for an occasion but may make his own. Are the enterprises of Alexander and Cesare, which are to be spoken of in a more secret room, the same as the enterprise of Cyrus?

Chapter VIII tells even more about the character of that enterprise; it is the clearest presentation thus far of what is required of the prince who is training himself for this enterprise. The chapter is on criminal founders, and it suggests what the character is of the founder or the most excellent captain, combining as he does virtue and wickednesses.

Chapter IX shows the ally of the prince, or the matter that is to sustain him. That matter—the people, or the many—sustains him in several senses, one of which is that it justifies him and his enterprise. Machiavelli chooses the end of the people over that of the aristocracy. He is the first political philosopher to turn to the many instead of the few as the basis of rule.

Chapter X is about fortresses and civil religion, a further indication of the significance of the turn to the people. The choice is put before the prince once again: either fortresses or the people. The people are a better defense than any fortress, for to have a fortress is not to be able to make a day of it, that is, not to be able to stand up to necessity or to provide for the relief of the human condition.

Chapter XI shows more fully what a fortress signifies, for the chapter speaks of the principate that does not govern and does not defend and then goes on to speak of the way in which the pontificate has come to power. Again a double meaning is suggested. On the one hand, the enemy is indicated, for the war is against an invisible or spiritual power. On the other hand, the pontificate has itself taken arms and has learned to wage war in the temporal order. If the spiritual order can learn how to take up arms, what can the temporal order learn? Can it learn how to resist this principate?

. . .

The third section, chapters XII through XIV, is about arms and religion, or the connection between faith and being armed or disarmed. The liberation of Italy is at the same time the arming of Italy. The highest kind of human being is now a captain. We have reached the height of the book, for we are speaking of the highest things. The greatest captains, however, are the writers. The warfare is a spiritual warfare; the war may even be described as a war of texts, or a war deciding which book shall rule the souls of human beings.

. . .

Chapters XV through XIX are about the qualities of the prince, or the one who is first; what we learn is that the qualities of the prince can arise not from that which is excellent in itself but from the requirements or limitations of matter or of the people. The new man is to be formed in terms not of the best but of what is universal, of what can be said not of a few but of all. Chapter XIX, the concluding chapter in this section, reveals the nature of the prince and therefore also reveals what is required by the enterprise or the conspiracy. We learn of other things, as the chapter promises, among which is how the rule of Roman emperors is like that of the Turk and therefore like that of Cyrus. The kingdom of Cyrus is the destroyer of the free life, and the Romans ruled as Cyrus ruled. Hence we stand with Philopoemen and Philip of Macedon in the war against the Romans.

. . .

Chapters XX through XXV deal with the prudence of the prince, for if virtue arises not from excellence but from necessity, then it is prudence—not blood, or virtue, or anything else—that, above all, characterizes the prince and makes one a prince. With chapter XXV we see what the rule of prudence means and how the prudent one conceals his prudence by teaching about impetuous action. The book concludes with the conquest and the promise of glory, a conquest that is made easy by matter, the occasion, fortune, God, and Machiavelli.

. . .

The first theme of *The Prince* is that of understanding acquisition and conquest as an enterprise. The Machiavellian enterprise is the knowledge of causes, and one can come to know a province only by conquering it. Hence the beginning of coming to know Italy is to acquire it or to rule it.

The ally in this new enterprise or conquest of Italy is the people. The many, or the *demos,* or the multitude, or the people (but never the "masses") are said, for the first time in political philosophy, to be at least equal to, if not even better than, the great, or the few, or the nobles, or the excellent. Machiavelli's teaching is that all men are equal, but only in terms of desiring or of all being equally in need, not because they are rational beings. The choice for the people leads to a new understanding of the virtues, and therefore of human nature. The human being is half man and half beast, not half man and half divine.

The true conquest is that of nature and necessity. At the deepest level, Machiavelli indicates that that is to be a new understanding of nature; hence a new prudence is also indicated. For the first time in the history of human thought, the possibility of an armed prudence is suggested. Machiavelli, in seeking to restore political prudence, declares that prudence must be armed. Understanding is no longer simply the understanding of the nature of things; it is the understanding of defenses and offenses. The philosopher is the unarmed Socrates who will not rule unless the people come to him; he is to be replaced by an armed movement headed by Machiavelli and his sons. Never again will the prudent be defeated and driven from the field, as was Philip of Macedon. Instead, they are to rule. They will rule by showing human beings how to conquer fortune, chance, and necessity, by building the ordered virtue, the dikes and dams, that will save them from the motions of matter. Prudence armed will give arms to all mankind against the variations or vicissitudes of chance—or at least prevent mankind from turning to illusions that disarm it.

Finally comes the call to reconquer the fatherland, to regain the kingdom of this world. That call is also a call for spiritual warfare, for a war of texts in which Machiavelli puts up his book to challenge the Book. That is the true war, the enterprise for which Machiavelli prepares the prince.

INDEX

Achaeans, 110, 121
Achaemenids, 20
Achilles, 67–68, 88
Aetolians, 15, 110, 121–22
Africa, 109
Agathocles, tyrant of Syracuse, 37, 38, 39, 64, 97–98, 112
Alcibiades, 11
Alexander III, the Great, king of Macedon, 11, 17, 19, 21, 60, 65, 67, 81, 97
Alexander VI, pope (Rodrigo Borgia), 33, 39, 42, 50, 61, 87, 138
Anastaplo, George, 42n.2
Angevins, 58
Anglo, Sydney, ixn.2
animo, 27, 28, 34, 39, 43–45, 55, 68, 83, 94, 98, 106, 121
Antiochus II the Great, king of Syria, 66, 110, 119
Aragon. *See* Ferdinand the Catholic
Aristophanes, 63
Aristotle, 9, 10, 46, 55, 56, 65, 67, 76, 79, 88, 92
arms, 25, 32–34, 56–57, 59–64, 71, 86, 92, 94, 103, 104–8, 117, 119, 133–35, 138–39
Art of War, The, 71n.3
Asia, 19–21, 24, 137
Athens, 22, 25, 121–22, 124
Augustine, 29, 89

barons, viii, 20, 22
Bentivogli, 92–93, 96
Bible, Biblical, 19, 20, 21n.6, 27, 69, 83, 131, 199, 203
blood, 12, 17, 18, 23, 83–84, 93, 98, 118, 139
Bloom, Allan, 90n.2
Bologna, 141
Borgia, Cesare, 4, 30, 32, 33, 42, 50, 61, 63–64, 82, 94, 96, 107, 130, 132

Borgia, Rodrigo. *See* Alexander VI
Brittany, 34
Buondelmonti, Zanobi, 120
Burgundy, 34

Caesar, Augustus, 9, 93
Caesar, Julius, 9, 70, 80–81, 93, 97
Caliphate, 98–99
Canneschi, 93
captain, 30, 38, 39, 41–42, 57–58, 59n.2, 61, 64–66, 68–69, 71, 97, 117, 123, 138, 139
Caracalla, Antoninus, 95, 98
Carmignuola, count of (Francesco Bussone), 58
Carthaginians, 57
Chalcis, 166
chance, 58–59, 61, 125–26, 130, 133, 140
Charles VII, king of France, 62–63
Charles VIII, king of France, 14, 56, 104
chase, 86. *See also* hunt
Chiron the Centaur, 25, 39, 86, 130
Christendom, 116
Christian, 18, 29, 83, 89, 109, 116, 121–22
Christian empire. *See* Holy Roman Empire
Christian infantry, 135
Christianity, 28, 49, 68, 81, 83, 116, 123
Chrysantas, 86
church, 16–18, 29, 49–52, 56, 58–59, 61, 105. *See also* pontificate, pope
Cicero, Marcus Tullius, 70, 78
Cleomenes, 45
Commodus, Marcus, 95–96, 98
condottiere, 30, 91
conspiracy, 91–96, 98, 139
Constantinople, 60, 96
Cox, Richard H., 31n.1
cruelty, 40–41, 55, 64, 82–85, 95, 97–98, 109–13
Cynoscephalae, 123
Cyrus, kingdom of, 20–21, 70–71, 138–39.

See also Darius, kingdom of
Cyrus the Great, king of the Medes, 20, 21,
  24, 25, 27–31, 59, 64, 67, 69–71, 81,
  86, 97, 99, 133, 138–39

d'Este, Alfonso, Duke of Ferrara, 13
d'Este, Ercole, Duke of Ferrara, 13
Darius, kingdom of, 22, 23, 24, 36, 60, 67,
  99, 119, 137
Darius III, King of Persia 19, 20, 32, 67, 99
David, 61–64, 116, 124
Dido, 82, 94
Discourses, vii, 21n.5, 31n.9, 100n.2,
  119–24, 134
disputation, 12, 17, 57, 83
dominion, vii, viii, ixn.1

ecclesiastical principate, 48–51, 113
emperor, Christian, 176
Emperor, Holy Roman, 47, 48, 55, 58, 105,
  108, 115–17
Emperor, Roman. *See* Roman emperors
Emperor of Constantinople. *See* Orthodox
  Emperor
empire, 11n.2, 29
Empire, Holy Roman, 47
Epaminondas, 57

Fabius Maximus, Quintius (Cunctator), 85
factions, 42, 43, 103–4, 108, 113
fatherland, 23, 25, 37, 39, 46, 68, 135–36,
  140
Ferdinand the Catholic (III of Aragon and V
  of Castile), King of Spain 13, 58, 90,
  109–10, 112
Fermo, 23, 39
Ferrara, 13
Flamininus, Titus Quintius, 110, 120, 123
Florence, 23–24, 58, 60, 93, 104–5, 108, 137
Florentine Histories, 99n.1, 135
Fogliani, Giovanni, 39
Forlì, 107
Forlì, countess of, 107
form, 27–28, 30, 34, 45, 93, 131–32
fortresses, 23, 47, 58, 103, 107–8, 113, 138
Fortuna, 130
fortune, 4–5, 10, 16, 26, 27, 30, 32–34,

36–38, 44, 50–51, 60, 70, 87, 103, 105,
  110–11, 113, 124–27, 129–34, 138, 140
founder(s), 25, 28, 32, 58, 99, 132, 136
France, king of, 14, 15, 19, 20, 34, 36, 50,
  61, 112
France, kingdom of, 22, 62, 94, 109, 119
French, 14, 18, 50, 60, 62, 127, 134–35
friend(s), 44, 66, 71n.3, 83, 92, 106, 120, 132

Gascony, 34
Gaul, 20
Gentile, 20
German cities, 47–48, 55, 107–8, 119–20
German orders, 134
Germany, 47, 108
Ghibbeline, 105
Gibbon, Edward, 11n.1
Giovanna II, queen of Naples, 58
Goths, 62
Gracchi, 45
Granada, 109
great, the, 22, 35, 43–45, 59, 93–94, 96, 107,
  119
Greece, 15, 22, 23, 25, 32, 46, 60, 66, 110,
  119–24, 137
Guelf, 105

Hannibal, 84, 97
Herodotus, 20, 21n.6
Hiero II, tyrant of Syracuse, 30, 32, 38, 61,
  63–64, 119–21
Hobbes, Thomas, 63
Holy Roman Emperor. *See* Emperor, Holy
  Roman
Holy Roman Empire. *See* Empire, Holy Ro-
  man
Homer, 67–68
hunt, 66, 70, 137. *See also* chase

imperium, 9, 11n.2, 38–39, 50, 95, 119
Ionian princes, 32
Israel, 25, 27, 49, 62, 116, 132–33
Israelites, 25
Italy, ix, 11, 14–17, 19–21, 24–26, 29,
  32–34, 36, 50–51, 56, 58–59, 60, 65,
  66, 97, 104–5, 109, 115, 118–22, 125,
  127, 131, 133–35, 137–39

Jerusalem, 27
Jews, religion of, 62
Jews, Spanish, 109
Josephus, Flavius, 21
Julius Caesar, 109, 143
Julius II, pope (Giuliano della Rovere) 13,,
    33, 50–51, 60–61, 129
justice, 43, 80–82, 111

Klein, Jacob, 13n.3
kingdom of God, 113
knowledge, 4, 5, 16, 17, 18, 19, 20, 27, 32,
    66, 134–36

Leo X, pope (Giovanni de' Medici), 5n.2,
    51, 133
Liverotto. See Oliverotto da Fermo
Livy, Titus, 110
Lombardy, 134.
Lorenzo de' Medici. See Medici, Lorenzo
    de'
Louis XI, 62
Louis XII, king of France 15, 17, 24, 92, 111

magnificence, 3, 4, 16
Mandragola, 137
Mansfield, Harvey C., 125n.3, 136n.2
Marcus Aurelius, 32, 96–97
Marranos, 109, 113n.1
Marx, Karl, 29, 63
matter, 13, 18, 25–27, 33, 43–45, 75, 92, 99,
    103, 106, 111, 120, 125–27, 131, 134,
    138–40
Maximilian I, Holy Roman Emperor, 115
Maximinus, Caius Julius Verus, 95, 98
Medici, ix, 4, 13, 23, 114, 132–33, 135
Medici, Giovanni de'. See Leo X
Medici, Lorenzo de' (Duke of Urbino), 4, 5,
    10, 16, 33, 114–15, 132–33
Milan, 14, 58, 107, 112, 117–19
miracle, 18, 29, 36, 58, 60, 125, 132–33
mirrors of princes, 3, 77
modes, 117, 127–30, 134
Moses, 25–27, 30, 31, 64, 67, 97, 132–33,
    137

Nabis, tyrant of Sparta, 45–46, 50, 91

Naples, kingdom of, 58, 118, 134
natural prince. See prince, natural
nature, 3, 11–12, 20–21, 28–29, 32–33, 35,
    40, 46, 62, 69–71, 75, 83, 88, 97, 99,
    106, 108, 114, 124, 127–31, 139–40
necessity, 3, 4, 22, 29, 37, 56, 66, 75–76, 84,
    87, 99, 112, 117, 128–31, 138–40
neutrality, 109–12
Normandy, 34

Odysseus, 133
Old Testament, 48, 95
Oliverotto Euffreduci da Fermo, 23, 37, 39
Orco, Remirro de (Don Ramiro de Lorqua),
    35, 42, 78, 94
orders, 25, 28, 63, 134–35
orders and modes, 68
Orsini, Paulo, 40
Orthodox Emperor, 60, 62

parlement, 94
Paul, St., 49
people, the, 28–29, 33, 35, 42–47, 48, 59,
    80–81, 86–87, 89, 92–97, 99, 103, 107,
    110, 119, 124–25, 128–31, 135, 138–39
Perseus, king of Macedon, 120
Persia, 20, 25, 60, 86
Pertinax, Publius Helvius, 96
Petrarch, 136
Petrucci, Pandolfo, 114
Philip II, king of Macedon, 57, 63
Philip V, king of Macedon, 66, 119–24,
    139–40
Philopoemen of Megalopolis, 66, 110,
    120–21, 139
philosophers, 28, 70–71, 106
philosophy, 11, 71
Pisa, 23, 58, 60, 104
Pistoia, 104
Plato, 10, 67, 75–76, 88
Plutarch, 24n.5, 25, 57, 110
pontificate, 51–52, 98–99, 119, 138
pope, the, 13, 18, 33, 49, 50, 58, 99, 105,
    115–16, 119, 136
Porcari, Stefano, 136
prince, natural, 12–13, 17, 36, 113, 128, 137
princeps senatus, 9

prophet, 28, 29, 36, 65, 68–69, 83, 133, 136
province, 14–15, 17, 19, 20–21, 23, 27, 34, 70, 122, 133
prudence, viii, 28, 32, 34, 40, 45, 58, 61, 68, 83, 103, 109–18, 125–31, 133, 136, 139–40
Pyrrhus, king of Epirus 21, 24, 30
Pythagorean numerology, 63

religion, 28, 38, 59, 64, 82, 89, 97, 121, 128, 138
republics, 9, 10, 12, 22–24, 57, 66, 76, 78, 104, 107, 121
Richard III, 41
Romagna, 32, 34, 55
Roman emperors, 32, 94–99, 121, 139
Roman Empire, 16, 22, 62
Roman senate, 9, 85, 97
Romans, 15, 16, 21–24, 29, 46, 57, 62, 66, 110, 112, 119–24, 134, 138–39
Rome, 11, 16, 25, 29, 57, 62, 66, 97, 122
Romulus, 25–26, 28, 31, 59, 132
Rouen, Cardinal of (Georges d'Amboise), 17–19n.2, 27–28
Rovere, 52
Rucellai, Cosimo, 120

sangue, 12
Saul, 61–62, 64
Savonarola, Girolamo, 28, 56–59
Scali, Giorgio, 45, 142
Scipio Africanus Major, Publius Cornelius, 31, 69–70, 84–85
sect, 71, 105, 117
servitù, 4, 24n.4
servitude, 4, 20, 23, 24n.4, 39, 60
Severus, Lucius Septimius, 95–96, 99, 128
Sforza, Francesco, 11, 13, 32, 58, 65, 71n.1, 97, 117
Sforza, Giacomuzzo Attendolo, 58
Sforzas, 71n.1, 89, 101
Shakespeare, 11n.5, 19n.1
Siena, 114
Sinigaglia, 63
Sixtus IV, pope (Francesco della Rovere), 13
Socrates, 10–11, 124, 140
Spain, 17, 119

Spanish infantry, 134
Sparta, 22–23, 45, 57, 91, 121–22, 124
state, vii, viii, 4, 9–10, 12, 15–20, 25, 27, 32–34, 41, 45–46, 49, 55, 59, 65, 77, 87, 89–90, 93–95, 103–4, 112, 117–19, 128
Strauss, Leo, 21n.3, 31n.6
Sultan, the, 181
Swiss, 57, 121, 134
Syracuse, 38, 61
Syria, 167

Tacitus, Cornelius, 63
Thebes, 22, 57
theology, 28
Theseus, 25, 28, 31, 59
Thucydides, 78
Turk, the, 15, 19, 20, 23, 60, 67, 98–99, 119, 137–39. See also the Caliphate
Turkey, 21, 33
Tuscan, 77, 121–22, 124
Tuscany, 11, 66, 70, 77, 121, 134, 137
tyranny, 15–16, 23, 35
tyrant, 10, 22, 36, 92

usurper, 4, 13, 30

Vailà, 58
Valentino. See Borgia, Cesare
Venafro, Antonio da, 114
Venice, 17, 58, 104, 112
Virgil, 82–83, 94
virtue, 4, 10, 16, 26, 28, 30, 32, 33, 36–38, 40, 58, 62, 75–81, 85, 87, 97, 109, 126–28, 133–36, 139
Visconti, Bernabò, 109–10, 112
Vitelli, Paulo, 58, 117
Vitelli, Vitellozo, 40

war, 17–19, 64–66, 68, 70–71, 80–82, 108, 117, 137, 140
writers, writing, 30, 31, 68, 70, 75, 77, 84, 87, 89, 94, 106, 118, 123, 133, 136–37, 139

Xenophon, 21n.6, 30, 31, 44, 67–68, 86, 133

Zama, 85